Race to the Bottom

'In their searing critique of superficial antiracism, Shafi and Nagdee offer fresh insights into the ideas and actions of Britain's radical antiracist internationalism.'

—Adam Elliott-Cooper, author of *Black Resistance to British Policing*

'Finally, a book that cuts through all the liberal conceits about diversity, representation and privilege to reconnect with Britain's radical histories of antiracist struggle.'

—Arun Kundnani, author of *The Muslims are Coming!*

'A sharp piece of political analysis that provides encouragement and direction to a new generation of antiracist rebels. You can feel their sense of urgency in every page.'

—Liz Fekete, Director, Institute of Race Relations

'Fiery [...] A tour of British antiracism, explaining where it goes wrong and where it goes right, providing an irresistible invitation to mass, collective, and organised revolt.'

—Luke de Noronha, lecturer in Race, Ethnicity and Postcolonial Studies, UCL and co-author of *Empire's Endgame*

'A biting book that analyses the history of antiracist activism without romance or malice. A deep and energising call for us to act decisively on our present.'

—Gracie Mae Bradley, co-author of *Against Borders* and ex-Director of Liberty

'For everyone longing for that other tradition of antiracism – the one whose authors don't make it onto the Queen's Birthday Honours list – read this breathtakingly exciting account of how our enemies are the same, all the struggles are linked and how, together, we can and must remake an antiracism from below.'

—Gargi Bhattacharyya, author of *Dangerous Brown Men* and co-author of *Empire's Endgame*

'The antiracism of Shafi and Nagdee is thrillingly uncompromising in its recall of anti-capitalist, working-class and community-based but internationalist roots. A must-read for anyone invested in the utopic vision and promise that antiracism necessarily nurtures.'

—Sivamohan Valluvan, author of *The Clamour of Nationalism*

'The kind of radical refocusing we need, taking stock not only of how antiracism is being defanged, but also its promise of a global reckoning which changes everything. Every antiracist in Britain needs a copy.'

—Joshua Virasami, author of *How to Change It*

'At a time when antiracism runs the risk of being reduced to vibes and t-shirts, Shafi and Nagdee's distinctly radical and avowedly internationalist call to arms provides the necessary political education radicals need to make "those in power afraid again".'

—Alana Lentin, Professor of Cultural and Social Analysis, Western Sydney University and author of *Why Race Still Matters*

'A tour de force. By re-centring an internationalist anti-capitalism, Nagdee and Shafi recover some of the most important contributions of Black power and Third World liberation movements, reviving them for use by the current generation.'

—Dalia Gebrial, contributing presenter at Novara Media and co-author of *Empire's Endgame*

Outspoken by Pluto
Series Editor: Neda Tehrani

Platforming underrepresented voices; intervening in important political issues; revealing powerful histories and giving voice to our experiences; Outspoken by Pluto is a book series unlike any other. Unravelling debates on feminism and class, work and borders, unions and climate justice, this series has the answers to the questions you're asking. These are books that dissent.

Also available:

Mask Off
Masculinity Redefined
JJ Bola

Border Nation
A Story of Migration
Leah Cowan

Behind Closed Doors
Sex Education Transformed
Natalie Fiennes

Lost in Work
Escaping Capitalism
Amelia Horgan

Make Bosses Pay
Why We Need Unions
Eve Livingston

Tangled in Terror
Uprooting Islamophobia
Suhaiymah Manzoor-Khan

Feminism, Interrupted
Disrupting Power
Lola Olufemi

Burnt
Fighting for Climate Justice
Chris Saltmarsh

Split
Class Divides Uncovered
Ben Tippet

Race to the Bottom

Reclaiming Antiracism

Azfar Shafi and Ilyas Nagdee

First published 2022 by Pluto Press
New Wing, Somerset House, Strand, London WC2R 1LA

www.plutobooks.com

British Library Cataloguing in Publication Data
A catalogue record for this book is available from the British Library

ISBN 978 0 7453 4467 6 Paperback
ISBN 978 0 7453 4469 0 EPUB
ISBN 978 0 7453 4471 3 PDF

This book is printed on paper suitable for recycling and made from fully managed and sustained forest sources. Logging, pulping and manufacturing processes are expected to conform to the environmental standards of the country of origin.

Typeset by Stanford DTP Services, Northampton, England

Simultaneously printed in the United Kingdom and United States of America

Contents

Acknowledgements

There are probably more people and groups to whom we owe gratitude than pages in this book. This book is the product of years of conversations, discussions, rants, Whatsapp messages, Google docs, catch ups at pickets and protests, and late-night organising meetings.

We have learned so much from our comrades in movements for Palestine, campaigns against Prevent, organising against state violence and challenging securitisation. It is in these movements that we find hope which is crucial to the heart of any project. In that vein, thank you to everyone at Northern Police Monitoring Project, Abolitionist Futures, Nijjor Manush and all the various groups and campaigns we have been regularly or intermittently involved with. Each one has given us crucial insights to take forward. It would be remiss of us if we didn't mention the NUS Black Students Campaign, which was a political home to us and many others. We owe deep gratitude to all those we organised within these movements.

Thank you to Adam Elliott-Cooper, Asad Rehman, Chardine Taylor-Stone, Aviah Sarah Day, Shanice Octavia-McBean, Luke De Noronha and Gargi Bhattacharyya for sharing with us their searing analyses peppered throughout the book. Special thanks to Sita Balani, Aadam Muuse and Mohammed Mumit for helping critically think through some embryonic reflections years ago, which have been explored more thoroughly in this book. And major gratitude to Hajera Begum and Tanzil Chowdhury for providing valuable feedback on draft chapters.

ACKNOWLEDGEMENTS

Thank you to our friends, who although we will not list out, know exactly who they are and the place they hold in our lives.

We especially want to thank Neda, not only for giving us this opportunity but for sticking with us in the midst of constant change as we wrote this book. Thank you to the staff at Pluto Press, a publisher whose books have played a part in our political education – we are truly honoured to have this book among your publications.

To Hajera and Zainab, thank you for your eternal companionship and for forgiving the glare of our laptops as we wrote through so many nights. To our parents, we are so grateful for the values of justice you instilled in us, for the lessons you taught us and we owe you more than we can say in words. We pray this is something you are proud of.

To our siblings; Amina, Anisa, Aysha, Hamza, Numayr and Izhar we hope this book makes up partly for us running across the country for so many years. To Mohammed, Mariam, Khadija, Zahraah Noor, Zayn, Yusha and Safiyyah – we do all this and organise so you can grow up and old in a world more just than the one we currently occupy.

Most importantly we thank God, the most merciful, the most compassionate. We make dua our efforts are accepted and that they better the world around us for all of your creation.

Introduction

When we first sat down to sketch the outline of what became this book, the state of affairs in Britain seemed dire. The country was still reeling from the results of the 2019 General Election – with the British left drowning in acrimony as the Conservative Party, appearing close to implosion just years prior, consolidated an iron grip on power.

Meanwhile, in spite of the centrality of racism to the events of recent years in Britain, antiracist organising – our own political home as organisers – was awash with divisions and contradictions here. Popular discourse on antiracism betrayed a glaring lack of theoretical depth, too often reduced as it was to petty 'privilege' politics, anxieties over 'unconscious bias' or rival claims for better 'representation'.

As individuals, our own coming-of-age played out against a backdrop of mass upheaval: from the spiralling crisis set in motion by the 2007/08 crash, to the resuscitation of a mass British left; from the fragmentation of domestic political allegiances, to the vicious counter-offensive by the media and political class, capped off by the rise of Boris Johnson's neo-Thatcherite government.

Having been somewhat acquainted with modern British history, the developments of the 2010s appeared strikingly familiar to us. The rise and fall of these left and/or radical forces echoed back to the period from the late 1960s to the late 1970s, when two parallel political lines came into fierce battle in Britain. It was during this time that a renewed left – embodied by an increasingly militant labour movement, the 'New Left' and the emergence of Britain's Black Power movement – wrestled with the deeply racist revanchism of the Enoch Powell-inspired 'New Right', as the post-war political consensus began to unravel. Those forces of the left seared their mark on British history – even if the Black Power era has remained criminally under-documented.

But bitterness stains the pages of this history as it moves into the 1980s. The Thatcherite revolution domestically – alongside the crushing of the counter-hegemonic forces of the socialist bloc and the Third World movement on the world stage – all indelibly mark our present historical moment. It is one where forces of the left in Britain are still very much on the defensive, and whose political landscape is still haunted by the afterlives of Enoch Powell's paranoid imaginary.

But this book is not a treatise on defeat, nor do we seek to simply rehash the well-worn tale of Powell-ism and Thatcher-ism. Instead, we will hone in on a struggle that began to mature during this same period – one that is all too often left out of the story of the seminal 1960s and 70s in Britain. That is, the struggle between the two souls of antiracism: the radicalism of antiracist organisations that blossomed in Britain's Black Power era from 1967–81, and an 'Antiracism from Above', set in motion definitively after the urban uprisings of 1981.

Overdue a reckoning

Developments that took place over the course of writing this book forced us to reconsider our early conclusions and tempered our tone.

During this time, the mass Black Lives Matter-inspired upris-ings broke out across the world in response to the police killings of George Floyd and Breonna Taylor – including the largest antiracist demonstrations in British history. This was followed a year later by the global wave of solidarity with Palestinians facing down the latest assault by Israel – again seeing the largest pro-Palestine demonstration in British history. The rise of the 'Kill the Bill' movement against the Police, Crime, Sentencing and Courts Bill in May 2021 traced out a possible new path for antiracist and anti-state violence campaigns.

Meanwhile amid a glut of lacklustre literature on racism that has been churned out over recent years, a number of deeply important books on racism and antiracism in Britain were published – some of which we have been able to read, others which have sat tantalisingly on our bookshelves as we prepared this book, all of which we are certain will claim their rightful place in the canon. But despite the euphoria of these recent political breakthroughs and upsurges, we could still trace how often they ended up running aground on familiar issues – both ideological and organisational. It appears that every wave of antiracist demonstrations and every burst of movement energy ended up wrestling against powerful currents of individualism, opportunism, inter-ethnic animosity and empty liberalism.

What we saw was a historical strategy stirring into motion whenever the fragile status quo was contested – which we have termed 'Antiracism from Above'. Within the space of half a century, this was a strategy that managed a shift away from radical self-organised groupings of the Black Power era in favour of the diversity and race relations industry, which has left us unequipped to deal with the stark rise in racism over the last decade in Britain. Whereas strong left critiques have been leveraged at the emergence of 'girlboss' feminism, or the thoroughly liberalised form of queer politics that dominates today, comparatively less has been written about the antiracist equivalent – though this does appear to now be changing.

Perhaps mercifully, racism and the raw arithmetic of demographic figures has spared those of us in Britain from our Barack Obama-style equivalent: a Black face for the white power structure, a symbol to disarm and legitimise critiques of state racism. But propelled by the likes of the Black Lives Matter movements and the urgency with which liberalism is attempting to take hold of 'the race question', the time may well be approaching when we must contend with such a challenge here in Britain. In order to prepare ourselves for such developments, our firm belief is that 'antiracism' in Britain was long overdue a reckoning, and a recovery of its own rich history.

Far too often, discussions about issues of race, racism and antiracism among the left are painted in the broadest of strokes. Serious assessments about the role and practice (and limitations) of antiracism in left-wing spaces are either jealously guarded from scrutiny, or written off as the simple excesses of 'identity politics' – a lazy, thought-terminating cliche of a term which we consciously avoid using in this book.

Instead, this book aims to describe the mechanics of how the radicalism of the Black Power era was negated through 'Antiracism from Above'. We have tried to resist the temptations of simple cautionary tales – of marking the developments of the 1980s onwards down to the 'betrayal' of individual activists 'selling out'.

Rather, we sought to take seriously the political and historical landscape that activists navigated through in the 1980s, as well as today. That is to say, we wished to think through the possibilities and pitfalls that activists are forced to grapple with in periods of seismic political change.

Limitations

The ideas, themes and topics in this book stem from our own experiences and conversations over the years as organisers, from discussions with friends and comrades, and from the studious analysis and documentation undertaken by the thinkers and organisers of yesteryear. Perhaps more than any other individual, we owe an ideological debt of gratitude to the breadth of work by one of Britain's foremost intellectuals: the late Ambalavaner Sivanandan, former director of the Institute of Race Relations. If this book achieves nothing more than to inspire readers to explore the rich history of antiracist thought in Britain, such as Sivanandan's, it would have been worth writing.

This text is by design, a partial account of racism and antiracism in Britain. It focuses in large part on the Black Power movements which comprised African, Caribbean and South Asians in Britain – but this is certainly not to suggest that these are the only groups affected by racism in Britain, nor the only ones that have resisted it.

We also chose to write a book retracing history at a time when tendencies across the political spectrum seem to have become prisoners of the past.

Whether the revivalist visions of ethnonationalists, the liberals who pine longingly for their faded days of glory, or even blinkered by their affection for post-war social democracy – far too many take *yesterday* to be their political horizon. This book does not seek to romanticise the history we speak of or call for a simple retreat into it; we merely seek to extract it for the lessons it can offer for the struggles of today.

This book is certainly not intended to be the final word on either Britain's Black Power era or of the state of antiracism; its scope is necessarily constrained by word limits and our own limitations as thinkers. But we hope it will be a humble contribution to a broader conversation about how to reimagine an emancipatory and transformative antiracism that is grounded in the struggle for socialism.

Chapter 1

Race, racism and racialisation

> Racism never stands still. It changes shape, size, contours, purpose, function, with changes in the economy, the social structure, the system and, above all, the challenges, the resistances, to that system.[1] – A. Sivanandan

The empirical realities of racism are well known and, by now, well-rehearsed: from discriminatory differentials in income, quality of housing and unemployment levels facing non-white people,[2] as well as the enduring menace of police brutality, inhumane immigration controls and repressive 'national security' powers.

But recognising racism empirically is not necessarily the same as understanding it analytically. Likewise, 'naming' racism may

---

1 Ambalavaner Sivanandan, 'The contours of global racism', *Institute of Race Relations* (2002) https://irr.org.uk/article/the-contours-of-global-racism (last accessed October 2021).

2 We note that there are many different terms used to collectively describe people racialised as 'non-white', each with their own limitations. We ourselves make use of a number of these through the course of this book – unless specified, our usage of either 'people of colour', 'Black and brown', 'racialised' and 'non-white' are interchangeable. 'Black*' is used, mostly in historical reference, to denote the framework referred to as 'Political Blackness', referring to people of African, Asian and Caribbean descent in Britain. The politics of collective terminology is explored at various points in the book.

be cathartic, but it is not conclusive. How do we develop a framework in which to integrate variegated experiences of racism, and connect them to concrete processes of social control and exploitation – of the extraction of labour, of social exclusion, of dispossession or displacement?

Take the infamous case of Altab Ali, the Bangladeshi textile worker stabbed to death in East London by three teenagers in 1978, in an act of 'Paki bashing'. Are we to identify 'racism' only insofar as the individuals that drove the knife into Altab Ali's neck? What, then, becomes of the mass theft of wealth from his homeland by British colonial rule – which drove people like him to Britain for work in the first place?

Or for that matter the British politicians who denounced and decreed against this immigrant inflow from the ex-colonies, and placed the target on the back of those like Altab Ali. Or the capitalist class who had maintained urban industrial spaces like London's East End as zones of permanent squalor, and breeding grounds for racial resentment. Or the British labour market which confined Asians like Altab Ali to toil for long hours in industries like textile work – forcing him to walk home through the dark streets of Whitechapel that night.

Racism did not enter the equation once those three teenagers set eyes upon Altab Ali – it shaped the conditions that placed him in that corner of East London on that fateful night in 1978. Altab Ali was not just a victim of circumstance, but a casualty of history.

Defining and governing race

In turn, antiracism cannot be reduced to opposition to acts of racist violence, but must strive for a transformation of the conditions that enable and authorise racism in all its forms.

In the face of racism's unyielding violence, to tussle over the question of definitions may seem irrelevant, indulgent or even obscene.

But exactly how ideas of race, and thus racism, are conceptualised and mobilised in popular discourse today determines the priorities of antiracist organising, the forms that organising takes and the basis of solidarities that form as part of it.

Developing constructive definitions so often means piercing through the cloud of confusion and 'common-sense' knowledge about race and racism. Sometimes this is expressed in pithy, but politically barren slogans – such as 'racism equals prejudice plus power', which locates racism fundamentally within the realm of attitude. Elsewhere, race is conflated with characteristics such as ethnicity or skin colour, as if 'race' is as natural as complexion, or necessarily defined by pigmentation. And at other times, race and racism are considered apart from one another – as if to suggest that 'race' is fundamentally a neutral category that is merely disfigured by acts of racism.

These are all approaches we reject as incorrect or inadequate in various ways. In contrast we would present the following as working definitions:

> *Race* is a social system. It marks out the structural relationship of certain social groups to power and to processes of exploitation, and indexes divisions of labour and social control.
>
> *Racialisation* is a dynamic process that draws on physiological, cultural and social markers to determine the boundaries of 'races' – groups can be racialised downwardly (negatively) or upwardly, and the boundaries shift over time and space.

And therefore *racism* is an active process of locking groups within a wider social structure of exploitation by maintaining and defending the system of race, through the sheer exercise of power or policy.

Race and racism serve to consolidate power within the British state, as well as underwriting British imperialism abroad. These often work in tandem – for example in the way that dehumanising racism is used to justify British military aggression against people abroad, who are then subject to racism when they are forced to flee to Britain, before being integrated into the bottom rungs of the social system as refugees or immigrants by racialising border powers. Race is never innocent – it is differentiation for the purposes of domination. And if we accept this, then trying to decouple race from racism is a chicken-and-egg situation: racism is race in motion.

These are definitions of *race* and *racism* which stress the fact that they are politically, socially and geographically contingent dynamics, rather than stable; that they emerge from a messy configuration of physical markers, social characteristics and cultural symbols that are shaped and re-shaped by changes in political economy and geopolitics.

Race and racism are politically enshrined, culturally reinforced and reproduced through social practices. State laws (or supra-states like the EU) and policies determine the boundaries of races – such as laws of citizenship. The modes and institutions of British state racism – border control, policing and national security – are the glue that holds them together. Ideological representations of racialised groups are transmitted through cultural apparatus like the media – producing the tropes and stereotypes that become embedded as common sense. And 'street racism' by the likes of the far right acts as a guarantor of racial discipline in society – by both building popular consent for racist policies, and containing any antiracist resistance that challenges the racialised order of things.

The definitions of race, racism and racialisation that we have described are broad and somewhat abstract, and speak to the overarching imperatives of race as a social system. But as important as a macro-level analysis is, racism takes root within the soil of individual states' own histories and social structures. What then, are the specificities of race and racism in Britain?

In Britain the structuring logic that anchors race is determined in relation to the Britishness of the 'native'. Race is shaped by the boundaries of inclusion and exclusion from Britishness and the benefits which that status confers. It is determined first by immigration policies policing who is and is not allowed into the country, and who is accepted into or denied citizenship; and then by domestic policies of policing, surveillance and the labour market locking ethnic or social groups within particular roles in society.

As counter-intuitive as it may seem then, race and racism are not strictly about colour or culture, but about exploitation and social control – and in Britain these are inextricably tangled up with questions of class and citizenship. To take race and colour/culture as interchangeable mistakes the ideological raw material of race with the structural relationship that it demarcates. And it assumes that racial categories are naturally existing rather than manufactured by law or social policy. And finally, assuming that racism flows logically out of colour or culture is to falsely endow a descriptor of experience (the *what* of racism) with explanatory power (the *why*), and ends up trapped in a circular logic where racism becomes its own justification.

The laws or policies that govern race and racial categories can draw together or diffuse groups of people. The remaking of a British national identity from the 1830s tethered the English working class to their ruling elite as members of an Anglo-Saxon Protestant nation in opposition to Irish Catholic migrant workers, thereby undercutting working class solidarity.[3] Meanwhile, racist anti-immigration laws in Britain through the 1960s and 70s, for example, progressively excluded African, Asian and Caribbean people of the Commonwealth from the boundaries of British state citizenship – but in doing so, provided the basis for solidarity between these geographically and ethnically diverse groups as 'Black' communities.

In his book, *Traces of History,* the late scholar Patrick Wolfe compared the rigid binary of the 'one-drop rule' for categorising enslaved Africans as 'Black' in the US to the elaborate classificatory system for enslaved Africans in Brazil. He explained these differences with reference to the demographic dangers posed to respective European settlers of each country: 'Where one [US] promoted solidarity among a White majority, the other [Brazil] promoted fragmentation among a non-White majority.'[4]

In all these distinct cases, social differentiation was designed for the purposes of domination. Race is not, in the final instance, about colour but about the demands of land and labour, accumulation and extraction.

Mistaking the wood for the trees

What we commonly understand as 'races' or racial 'identities', then, are the avatars of evolving relations of power and exploitation that exist within the context of capitalist-imperialism. For us, race is fundamentally something one is subject to rather than something one possesses. But the way in which race is reduced to a simple matter of subjective identity in popular discourse

3 Satnam Virdee, *Racism Class and the Racialized Outsider*, (London: Macmillan International Higher Education/Red Globe Press, 2014), p. 30.

4 Patrick Wolfe, *Traces of History Elementary Structures of Race* (London & New York: Verso, 2016), p. 134.

flattens and erases the social and political forces that shape it. And in doing so, takes antiracism out of the directives of social transformation and into the realm of self-affirmation, or the subjective embrace of identity – two tasks which intersect, but are certainly not interchangeable. At worst it can slide into a reactionary politics.

When race is taken as primarily an identity, a lot of heat and light can be expended in trying to determine and police the boundaries of race, in order to decide who may and may not speak on issues of racism affecting certain groups – which sometimes devolves into very ugly spectacles. We can also see this echoed in the way that class is reduced to an identity in popular discourse, rather than in the political-economic sense of relationship to the means of production.[5] In turn, to be 'working class' becomes a matter of cultural markers – of accent, of culinary habit, of geography – rather than a signifier of social-economic power.

This paves the way for all manner of right-wing charlatans to perform a perverse caricature of what they deem 'authentic' working class existence and to mobilise the 'working class' for racist and reactionary ends. And finally, it leads to the curious compartmentalisation of the non-white working class: as if the 'white' worker of Britain is the default working class subject, ignoring that the dynamics of race and citizenship are always present in the creation of the working class as a social force – or as Satnam Virdee puts it, that 'race was constitutive in the making, unmaking and remaking of the working class in England'.[6]

But ultimately, we're far more interested in the question of what race does and what drives it, rather than just 'naming' something as racist. To be downwardly racialised in Britain

5 See: https://marxists.org/glossary/terms/c/l.htm (last accessed October 2021).

6 Virdee, *Racism Class and the Racialized Outsider*, p. 8.

means being subject to uneven patterns of exclusion and inclusion within social, political and economic life – which is to say the exclusionary experience of racism (social), disenfranchisement and fragile claims to citizenship (political), and of being concentrated within insecure, precarious or 'unskilled' strata of the job market (economic).

Policing and racism

Policing is central to the process of racialisation and the production of race.

But rather than the popular idea that policing and state violence is a reaction to already-existing racial groups, it is through policing that such racial hierarchies are bounded and maintained in the structure of society.

To put it another way, seeing British police officers as having an impulse to scope out and subject Black people to violence is simplistic. Rather, we see that one of the central roles of the police is to lock African-Caribbean communities into a social and economic structure in Britain which concentrates them largely within a site of exclusion and poverty. So too with immigration enforcement, which is bound up with the economic exploitation of non-citizens. The precise form of state violence may not be forever fixed – but as long as we live in a racially stratified society, such patterns of policing and exclusion will continue to play out on the lives of racialised people in order to manage that tiered system.

Any conversation of policing in Britain must factor in the three intertwined forms of state power: 'regular' police forces, immigration control and 'counterterror' or national security policing, and the multifarious ways that they operate together. For example, much of today's 'counterterror' arsenal draws on and deepens immigration powers of control and exclusion, and in turn it has augmented and militarised 'regular' policing through the gradual introduction of police arms under the pretence of countering terrorism.[7] These are the means through which the structural position of non-white people in society are marked out and managed, and through which their relationship with the state is mediated. Race in Britain is beaten into formation between police batons and policed borders.

The roots of British policing in various forms of social control of the repression of the working classes lend themselves well to the role of policing in the control of non-white people in Britain today. Building on his experience managing Britain's colonial occupation in Ireland, Robert Peel created the Metropolitan Police in 1829 – yet contrary to popular knowledge, this was not the first police force in Britain. The Marine Police Office was created 30 years earlier in 1798 under the leadership of Patrick Colquhoun, later known as the 'patron saint of the police institution'.[8] The MPO was established following a meeting of slavers in London concerned about the lifting of their slave-made goods and those extracted from the colonies by dockworkers in London.

Through the highly influential West India Planters and Merchants lobby, Colquhoun was able to garner political and media support for a police force to ensure working-class Londoners were unable to seize the goods of the slavers. Their support

7 For more on the history of modern counterterror powers in Britain, see Azfar Shafi, 'The 9/11 complex: The political economy of counter-terrorism', *Transnational Institute* (2021), https://longreads.tni.org/stateofpower/the-9-11-complex-the-political-economy-of-counter-terrorism (last accessed October 2021).

8 John Moore, 'Protecting the Property of Slavers: London's First State Funded Police Force', *Abolitionist Futures* (2021), https://abolitionistfutures.com/latest-news/protecting-the-property-of-slavers-londons-first-state-funded-police-force (last accessed October 2021).

in Parliament was particularly high, with over 70 MPs being planters,[9] and having seen off efforts to outlaw slavery in the Commons multiple times. This police force would target the livelihoods of London's working class and was explicit about its duty in protecting capital from the threat of working-class rebellion.

Returning to Robert Peel, his officers – the eponymous 'bobbies' on the beat – came to be seen as a necessary element of British society following the Peterloo Massacre in 1819, among other working-class uprisings. The success of their preceding force in Ireland in quashing uprisings led to their consolidation and later expansion worldwide,[10] as Alex Vitale documents in *The End of Policing*. Their initial duties were simple: to protect power by breaking strikes, beating protestors and protecting land – clearly, not much has changed.

It goes without saying that not all manifestations of racism are exactly alike – differently racialised groups are subject to different forms of racist exploitation, and serve different functions within a wider social structure. And the forms that racisms take are deeply shaped by dynamics such as class, gender, and other social oppressions. But we're wary of the increasingly popular notion that each manifestation of racism should be treated as distinct, discrete phenomena independent of one another – which can retreat into a form of tunnel vision, or 'oppression Olympics' that pits forms of racism against one another. Instead, we draw the conclusion that different racisms should be understood as part of a totality – as interlocking forms of exploitation

9 Christer Petley, *White Fury: A Jamaican Slaveholder and the Age of Revolution* (Oxford: Oxford University Press, 2018), p. 96.

10 For more on the origins of policing, see Chapter 2 of Alex S. Vitale's *The End of Policing* (London & New York: Verso, 2017), pp. 31–54.

that mutually reinforce and make possible other forms of racism within the landscape of capitalist society.

This is the case even when they operate in different ways. To give an example, the different forms of policing described above – 'regular', immigration and national security – can either be analysed independently of one another, in terms of *which* specific social groups are disproportionately targeted by them, and in *what ways* they are brutalised by them. Or they can be analysed as the multiple, interconnected faces of state power that feed into one another, and must be tackled together even if they operate at degrees apart.

Amrit Wilson illustrates how this shared understanding existed within movements of the 1970s, at the outset of her book *Finding a Voice: Asian women in Britain*. There she reflects on how, for African-Caribbean and Asian people organising then,

> Our experiences of racism...[were] similar or dialectically linked. While under the notorious SUS law young African-Caribbean men were harassed with frequent stop and searches and often violently arrested, on suspicion of the intent to break the law, Asians were arrested, detained and sometimes deported because they were suspected of being illegal immigrants.[11]

Touching on the decision by the Organisation of Women of African and Asian Descent (OWAAD) to campaign against invasive virginity tests at airports despite them being directed predominantly against South Asian women, Nydia A. Swaby explains that

---

11 Amrit Wilson, *Finding a Voice: Asian Women in Britain* (Quebec: Daraja Press, 2018).

> Though this issue did not directly affect all black women, for OWAAD, virginity testing was part and parcel of Britain's highly racialised and gendered immigration policies targeted at dividing black families and subjugating black women.[12]

An antiracism that is merely reactive to specific *forms* of racism,[13] or which tackles these forms in isolation, ends up like the parable of the blind men and the elephant: partial, incomplete and incoherent. If antiracist politics is to become a hegemonic power bloc, rather than a fragmented mosaic of movements, then it needs an analytical framework that is attentive to the *function* of racisms as different parts of a totality, and hones in on the exploitation underpinning it.

Boundaries of Britishness[14]

When it comes to analysing the social structure of Britain, then, the concepts of race, citizenship and class are deeply interwoven.

Britain's racial framework has been largely shaped by the many lives of British imperialism: its transformation from empire into the modern British state during the twentieth century, its absorption into what is now the European Union and its recent break. Through this process of transformation, the global division of 'white' Britons in the metropole governing crown subjects in the colonies was reorganised by a series of laws into an internal hierarchy of citizens and various classes of migrants within the British state. This particular imperial history, as well

12 Nydia A. Swaby, 'Disparate in Voice, Sympathetic in Direction': Gendered Political Blackness and the Politics of Solidarity', *Feminist Review*, 108:1, (2014), pp. 11–25.

13 For example, by considering issues of Islamophobia, anti-Black racism, anti-Asian racism and so on as exclusive of one another.

14 With thanks to Luke de Noronha for his comments here.

as international laws and treaties to which Britain was bound, ensured that much of its non-white migrant population tended to be asylum seekers or 'economic migrants', who were slotted into the bottom rungs of British society, beneath its native working class. This contrasts with the laws and politics selectively governing migration to the US from the 1960s onwards, which – very roughly speaking – created a bifurcation between middle class migrants who served as a 'buffer class' for native non-whites, and dispossessed asylum seekers, including from neighbouring American and Caribbean countries.

The UK border is a system of legal exclusion that is integral to the formation of race and racism. It is the dividing line for Britain's racial framework and over time has created the variegated classifications of citizen, subject, asylum seeker, refugee, alien and foreign national. Out of this, Britain has developed a racialised classificatory system of concentric circles, with: 'white' British natives at its core, native non-whites outside that, 'economic migrants' outside that, and refugees/asylum seekers on the periphery of Britishness[15] – and with each of these circles marked by their own internal subdivisions.[16]

Citizenship is power, it regulates the relationship to Britishness that is central to British racial construction. But as a juridically defined status, citizenship in Britain is an inherently political and elastic category. Therefore the boundaries

15 This is not to say that there is a single straight line between citizenship status and deprivation, or to deny that there are individuals and groups of migrants which ascend to the heights of British society. But we don't believe that this fact undermines this overall racial framework any more than the fact that certain working-class people can 'make it' out of poverty undermines the fact that class oppression structures society, either.

16 The relatively privileged status (until recently) afforded to migrants from the European Economic Community/the EU marked their experience out in distinction to other groups of migrants whose passage into Britain was made even more precarious and exploitative, for example.

of citizenship can be adapted to serve political demands. The Immigration Act 1971 infamously linked the 'right of abode' in Britain to the concept of 'patriality', in effect privileging those from the 'Old Commonwealth' – i.e. the British settlers of New Zealand, Australia, Canada, etc – at the expense of those from the 'New Commonwealth' – i.e. the formerly colonised Caribbean, Pakistanis, Indians, etc.

The elastic nature of citizenship is also reflected in mainstream ideas about the boundaries of Britishness, which tend to operate like a carousel – with certain groups being alternately drawn in, and pushed out of the boundaries of Britishness over time. Since the Rushdie Affair of 1988/89 – demonstrations against Salman Rushdie's book, *The Satanic Verses*, due to blasphemous references to the Prophet Muhammad – discourse around the predominantly Pakistani and Bangladeshi Muslims in Britain has taken on a distinct character. It has framed them in terms of either their foreign-ness as migrants, or in the case of British-born citizens, as cultural outsiders in Britain who lie beyond the boundaries of Britishness. Since the turn of the twenty-first century and the growth of the national security apparatus, this discursive framing of Muslims in Britain has been coupled with an expanding array of state powers to exclude and deport individuals, centring largely on Muslims.

Recent cases of long settled non-white citizens of Britain being deported, or of expanding powers to strip the citizenship of individuals – up to and including British-born citizens such as Bengali schoolgirl Shamima Begum – only serve to underscore how fragile British citizenship and the nature of inclusion within Britishness is, especially for non-white people. And what better to illustrate the deeply colonial nature of these relationships than the fact that powers like citizenship stripping are legally justified on the basis of individuals 'not being conducive to the public good': in other words, that *coloured folk* who don't take enough effort to fit in as good citizens in Britain can find themselves expelled.

Dynamic configurations of race, class and citizenship buttress British capitalism and imperialism. As a potent social force, racism has been able to bind together both the dispossessed and the dominant. As described above, in the case of Britain historically, this has meant drawing together sections of the 'white working class' and the white elite in an unequal embrace of race and the nation. For the latter, racism serves as a buffer to protect their social position. The former, meanwhile, can be drawn towards a reactionary defence of racialised hierarchies in order to make claims for social advancement; for example, through the idea that they are *deserving* of social welfare while their foreign and/or downwardly racialised counterparts are not.

Now, non-white British citizens have been able to make similar claims against non-natives. An example of this is the Taking the Initiative Party, launched as a Black-led political party in the aftermath of the 2020 Black Lives Matter wave of demonstrations.

Coming off the back of mass protests against British state racism, the party's initial 'manifesto' evinced a studious emphasis on reorienting British policy to better serve its *citizens* first and foremost. It was through this feint that the party could speak of being 'bold in our expression of change' while echoing Conservative Party talking points to a tee – including by 'taking a firm stance on limiting migrant access to public funds and [seeking] to deport anyone who enters the UK purely to gain access to these resources'.[17]

At a more everyday level, this notion of deserving/undeserving migrants is also expressed in the way that some longer-estab-

17 https://theinitiativeparty.org.uk/our-party (last accessed June 2021).

lished migrants can validate their position in society on account of being 'good', productive immigrants, as opposed to supposedly feckless newcomers.

The price to pay for entry into the nation is allegiance to racialised notions of Britishness. The social cost is broken solidarities and a fatally divided working class.

Chapter 2

Rise of Black Power in Britain

> Who are they?
> They are those immigrants who live off the labour of other immigrants, making contacts on the way with state power and the labour movement, with MPs, with councillors, with organised business, with the political hustlers who pose as representatives of the white community. – *Race Today* journal[1]

The rise of Black Power

It is through this understanding of racism's role that we can make sense of the fact that in times of crisis, racism becomes more acute – because these crises bring into sharper relief the already-racialised structure of society. It also explains why, once economic crises harden into generalised social crises, 'legitimate working class grievances' so often end up reflecting ruling class racism.

These dynamics of race, class and citizenship collided in the late 1960s, as the post-war settlement – of social democracy, the welfare state and Keynesianism – entered a period of terminal crisis that would make way for the emergence of neoliberalism.

1 Paul Field, Robin Bunce, Leila Hassan & Margaret Peacock, *Here to Stay, Here to Fight: A Race Today Anthology* (London: Pluto, 2019), p. 112.

As the crisis matured, two parallel political lines emerged which offered two very different visions of what Britain could become.

On one hand was the rise of Powellism, a deeply reactionary strain of white English nationalism that sought the end of immigration to Britain. Powellism shot to national attention in April 1968 with then-Tory Cabinet member Enoch Powell's infamous 'Rivers of Blood' speech in Birmingham. Powell's incendiary address, haunted by fever dreams of a Britain being colonised by the darker races, struck a chord across the country. Powellism provided the intellectual scaffolding for what would be known as Britain's New Right through the 70s – which eventually consolidated power with the rise of Margaret Thatcher's Conservative government in 1979.

On the other hand, the birth of Britain's Black Power era was marked by the formation of the Universal Coloured People's Association (UCPA) in 1967, and a constellation of groups, formations and campaigns following it. This era heralded the radicalisation of African, Caribbean and Asian communities in Britain – who had long been excluded from the fruits of the post-war settlement despite comprising the labour force that underwrote it – and produced the most vibrant period of antiracism in Britain's modern history.

Black Power emerged as a response to growing racism in British society. But more significantly, it was the political expression of the most alienated sections of post-war Britain: of those that had been incorporated into the very bottom of its working class, its racial hierarchy, of Britishness, and who had been excluded from the institutions of British society. Black Power represented both a political rupture and a generational break.

The 1967 visit of US-Trinidadian Black Power leader Stokely Carmichael (later Kwame Ture) to speak at the London Dialectics of Liberation conference inaugurated Black Power in Britain. It resulted in the formation of UCPA and an array of organisations subsequently – the British Black Panther Movement, Black Unity and Freedom Party (BUFP), Black Workers Movement (BWM), Organisation of Women of African and Asian Descent (OWAAD), Black Liberation Front (BLF), Race Today Collective, Awaz, the Black Peoples' Alliance (BPA), the Asian Youth Movements (AYMs), the Fasimbas and countless others.

The work undertaken by these groups was diverse, and the priorities of specific groups operating under the Black Power banner reflected their own particular encounters with British racism. For Africans and Caribbeans this often centred on countering police violence and police attacks on African-Caribbean social spaces. African and Caribbean women often led on defence campaigns for individuals targeted by the forces of law and order, as well as on alternative or supplementary schooling programmes. African-Caribbean and Asian women organised around issues of family and reproductive justice such as experimental use of the Depo-Provera contraceptive on African-Caribbean women. Asians at large confronted anti-migrant powers, while Indians in particular were remarked upon as being the most militant sector of the labour force, with longer-established organisations like the various Indian Workers Associations (IWAs) engaging in industrial action against racist employers. Meanwhile, Bangladeshi political action centred on self-defence against racist attacks, as well as a powerful squatters movement in East London.

As a youthful movement, it largely compromised second-generation Commonwealth migrants – or rather, first generation citizens of the British state – and signalled a departure from the more moderate and conciliatory antiracism led by middle-class sections of their parents' generation. These had taken the form of various immigrant and welfare associations that had ossified into semi-appendages of local government, in order to manage migrant populations. They also included institutions like the toothless local Community Relations Commissions set up under the Race Relations Act 1968, where migrants and white liberals worked together alongside local government representatives and police.

This new assertiveness was captured in a 1978 journal entry by Pratibha Parmar, then an activist in the Bradford Black Collective, reporting on a national demonstration against immigration laws:

> The time has long since gone when blacks in Britain could afford to make pleas to the British government that it honour its moral obligations to us and grant us our full rights. We should not be fighting a moral crusade, begging to be allowed to live as equal citizens.[2]

Meanwhile, the generational break was illustrated dramatically in places like Southall, West London. In 1976, the Southall Youth Movement was born after the youth outflanked the moderate and well-established IWA (Southall) to call a march, street occupation and de-arrest following the racist murder of Sikh teenager Gurdip Singh Chaggar in early June that year.

Differently, but equally dramatic, was the example of the Institute of Race Relations (IRR) – initially founded by Chatham House as an elite-oriented think tank, saturated with corporate funding, to ponder on the 'problems' posed by non-white communities in Britain. In 1972, in the midst of the new radi-

---

2 Pratibha Parmar, 'Against Immigration Laws', *Race Today*, 10:7, (November/December 1978), p. 149. https://archive.leftove.rs/documents/ADEP/1 (last accessed August 2021).

calisation of those communities, the IRR was transformed into a radical hub of antiracist thought by a 'palace coup' led by its staff.

The socialism of the slums

Having long been banished to the blind spots of the British post-war settlement, it is over the course of struggles from the late 60s onwards that an increasingly militant Black and brown working class came to assert themselves as a political force in Britain. They confronted both the racialised division of labour that structured industry on the basis of their exploitation, as well as the brutal policing that structured social life, and sought to suffocate forms of community and cultural resistance.

Many, though by no means all, of the groups and figureheads which emerged in the Black Power era espoused some form of socialism – from the Marxism-Leninism of the Black Unity and Freedom Party to the more organic, at-times ambiguous, socialism professed by Sivanandan, and even the libertarian socialism of the Race Today Collective.

Yet they often had a fraught relationship with Britain's 'white left', whom they indicted for their blind spot on racism and xenophobia at home, and for having largely ceded their opposition to British imperialism.[3] For decades, this had been a left that professed a 'radical' vision of Britain which, it seemed, was curiously unblemished by the question of Blackness.

The response was that most of the Black Power groups self-organised and found strength among themselves – as caucuses

3 The record of the 1945–50 Labour Government is the quintessential example of this phenomenon. See for example, Alfie Hancox, 'Lieutenants of imperialism: social democracy's imperialist soul', *Review of African Political Economy* (2021), https://roape.net/2021/07/15/lieutenants-of-imperialism-social-democracys-imperialist-soul (last accessed August 2021).

or organisations of Africans, Caribbeans and Asians – rather than within white-led institutions like the Labour Party.[4]

Organising themselves through workers committees, unions, community associations, campaign groups as well as looser formations, they came into open conflict with the primary institutions reproducing racism in British society – politicians, private profiteers and policing – as well as the secondary institutions that buttressed them. These included the education system, the healthcare system, the media and the white labour movement – with their deeply ingrained chauvinism, and their role as gatekeepers of a compromise politics with the Labour Party.

This period underscored how central antiracism was to labour organising, and how labour organising was a key site of antiracist action, rendering the timid paternalism of Community Relations Committees and their ilk ever more irrelevant. The watershed Mansfield Hosiery Strikes in Loughborough, 1972, boldly underlined this message.

The strike by mainly Asian men and women workers at the factory was conducted in the face of racism and reactionary manoeuvring by the local trade union, whose offices the strikers had to occupy before the strike was declared official. They also had to contend with meddling by the local CRC and Race Relations Board, who were described as 'moving to find a new lease of life in the mediating machinery within industry and [presenting] an image of management with a liberal face'.[5]

---

4 In turn, they were accused – with varying degrees of tactfulness – by sections of the left for being 'divisive', and prioritising 'separatism' over the class struggle for socialism.

5 Bennie Bunsee, 'Women in Struggle: The Strike at Mansfield Hosiery', *Spare Rib*, 21, (March 1974), p. 18, https://archive.leftove.rs/documents/ESE/19, (last accessed August 2021).

The strike forced the Department of Employment to intervene, and the strength of the campaign emboldened a developing movement of Black and Asian workers, who tapped into reservoirs of support among their local communities rather than relying on the trade union machinery – a strategy deployed later at strikes such as the Imperial Typewriters Strike of 1974. Leaflets distributed by the Black Workers Movement at a conference on trade unions and racism called by the strike committee crystallised the lessons learned from examples like Mansfield, which included:

> 1. Mobilising the strength of the whole Black class in the community and in the factory. 2. Seeking to talk directly to the white workers and demanding they support our struggles (as we give ours) in their own class interest. But refusing to concede to racist hostility if they refuse. 3. Internationalising our struggle wherever possible.[6]

The strength of the Black* and migrant-led strikes during this decade stood out against the malaise creeping into a society sinking into crisis. They forced white trade unionists to reassess the myopia of their militancy; of the dangers of ignoring those whose exploitation underpinned the economy at large. This in turn meant that certain trade unions had to rethink the nature of their political compact with the Labour Party who helped maintain this hierarchy of domination, and which in time could have forced them to more fundamentally reconsider their place within the structure of British society: were they to continue as custodians of a racist social contract, or act as co-conspirators in its downfall?

6 Ron Ramdin, *The Making of the Black Working Class in Britain* (London & New York: Verso, 2017), p. 365–6.

Black Power is not an island

Black Power in Britain was informed as much by the US movement from which it took its name as by the anti-imperialist ferment then sweeping the part of the world once known as the 'Third World'.[7] From decolonisation struggles across Africa, the tenacious Vietnamese resistance to the US war machine, battles against Zionist and imperialist domination in the 'Middle East', the revolutionary developments in socialist Cuba and China and the emergence of the Non-Aligned Movement political bloc[8] – the Third World shone as the lodestar of liberation in the latter twentieth century.

Black Power was not just an expression of domesticated 'British' radicalism, it reflected the militancy of formerly colonised people on the move through history. This was infused into Black Power organisations – many of whom didn't simply speak about anti-imperialism, but baked it into their constitutions. The aims and objectives of the OWAAD, for example, committed them to '[S]upport all anti-imperialist struggles and national liberation movements fighting against colonial and neo-colonial domination...[and] to forge close links with all the other anti-imperialist and anti-colonial struggles and organisa-

---

7 Despite being frowned upon today as a term denoting wretchedness, 'Third World' was used during this time as a symbol of anticolonial political power and agency. See Vijay Prashad's *The Darker Nations* and *The Poorer Nations* for the history of the Third World project and its decline.

8 The Non-Aligned Movement (NAM) refers to the political bloc of states that maintained a position of formal independence from both the NATO powers and the Soviet bloc during the Cold War. The NAM emerged out of the 1955 Bandung conference in Indonesia, and consolidated itself at the 1961 conference in Belgrade, the former Yugoslavia.

Drawing together much of the formerly colonised countries of the world, the NAM functions as a broad front for national sovereignty and independent development, including through multilateral forums like the United Nations.

tions',[9] while the IWA-GB's objectives included '[Supporting] the national liberation struggles of the Asian, African, and Latin American people and co-operate with other organisations working for the same end.'[10]

The newly radicalised IRR also reflected this new internationalist sensibility, by relaunching its house journal, *Race & Class*, with the tagline 'Journal for Black and Third World Liberation', while the *Race Today* magazine covered movements across the likes of the Caribbean, India and in Britain's first colony: Ireland.

This internationalist sensibility harkened back to an earlier era in which Britain was a base for the circulation of anticolonial revolutionaries from its then-colonies. In 1945, Manchester played host to the Fifth Pan-African Congress, which saw 87 delegates from 50 organisations across the world descend on the city for a series of debates, discussion and strategising sessions towards the liberation of the African continent. In attendance were three future presidents: Hastings Banda of Malawi, Jomo Kenyatta of Kenya and Kwame Nkrumah of Ghana along with notable scholars and activists such as W.E.B. Du Bois, C.L.R James, Amy Garvey, George Padmore and more. The Congress would prove seminal, underlining the importance of destabilising British imperialism through the collaboration of subjugated and colonised peoples all across the continent and the world. In the words of Nkrumah, 'Congress was a tremendous success [. . .] (it) advised Africans and those of African descent to organise themselves into political parties, trade unions,

9 'OWAAD Draft Constitution' (c.1978), DADZIE/1/1/2, *Stella Dadzie Papers*, held at: London: Black Cultural Archives.

10 'Indian Worker', no. 1, (1973), MSS 217/B12/3/5, *Socialist Reproduction, 1915–1976 collection*, held at: Coventry: Modern Records Centre.

co-operative societies and farmers' organisations in support of their struggle for political freedom and economic advancement.'[11]

In the late 1960s, this deeply internationalist and anti-imperialist consciousness was crystallised in the signature framework of Black Power, commonly known today as 'Political Blackness' (denoted in this book as Black*), which defined 'Black' in opposition to the global white power structure. Today, Political Blackness is often invoked, but rarely understood – at best written off as a peculiar artifact of British history. But the development of Black* as a political, rather than phenotypical, signifier in the late 1960s cannot be decoupled from other strains of anticolonial and/or anti-imperialist thought circulating at the time.

Towards the end of his life, Malcolm X articulated an anti-colonial solidarity around the emerging 'black revolution . . . taking place in Africa and Asia and Latin America; when I say black, I mean non-white—black, brown, red or yellow.'[12] The particularities of the Caribbean political and ethnic context from which many Black Power activists in Britain hailed is also important:[13] Guyanese Marxist Walter Rodney put forward an expansive conception of 'Black' rooted in a global analysis of power – referring to those who were 'not obviously white . . . and are excluded from power. The black people of whom I speak, therefore, are . . . the hundreds of millions of people whose

11 Kwame Nkrumah, *Ghana: The Autobiography of Kwame Nkrumah* (London: Panaf, 1973), p. 127.

12 Malcolm X, 'The Black Revolution', (1964) Available at: https://malcolmxfiles.blogspot.com/2013/07/the-black-revolution-april-8-1964.html (last accessed August 2021).

13 This is explored further in John Narayan's excellent 2019 journal article in *The Sociological Review* 'British Black Power: The anti-imperialism of political blackness and the problem of nativist socialism', *The Sociological Review*, 67:5, (2019), pp. 945–67.

homelands are in Asia and Africa, with another few millions in the Americas'.[14]

Meanwhile in its cultural output the Cuban Organization of Solidarity with the People of Asia, Africa and Latin America (OSPAAAL) riffed off the Black/white binary of contemporary US Jim Crow as a 'metonym not for a global color line but for a Tricontinental power struggle in which all radical, exploited people, regardless of their skin color, are implicated'[15] – with white authority symbolising empire, and Black people symbolising resistance. And in an address to the British Black Panther Movement in July 1968, venerable Pan-Africanist and former Ghanaian President Kwame Nkrumah stated that 'By Black Power we mean the power of the four-fifths of the world population which has been systematically damned into a state of underdevelopment by colonialism and neo-colonialism'.[16]

A network of bookshops, publishing houses and reading groups – some independent, others associated with political organisations – gave Black* people in Britain an insight into the revolutionary stirrings afoot in distant lands. Literature on the US Black Power movement and on the national liberation struggles enabled Britons to place themselves within a wider global framework of struggles against capitalism and imperialism that was bound up with the struggle against white racism.

In this way, as much as 'Political Blackness' reflected a desire for non-white unity and solidarity *within* Britain, it also symbolised an anti-imperialist understanding of *global* power.

14 Walter Rodney, *The Groundings With My Brothers* (London & New York: Verso, 2018), p. 10.

15 Anne Garland Mahler, *From the Tricontinental to the Global South: Race, Radicalism, and Transnational Solidarity* (Durham: Duke University Press, 2018), p. 13.

16 'Message to the Black People of Britain by President Kwame Nkrumah' (1968), MSS 149/2/2/5, *Papers of Bob Purdie (b.1940), socialist and trade unionist, 1927–1977*, held at: Coventry: Modern Records Centre.

Certainly, it may appear unintelligible today. But perhaps, more than anything else, this reflects the eviction of anti-imperialism from the antiracist register.

Policing the crisis

The gradual, uneven convergence of forces on the left around the question of racism was met by a convergence of the governing classes around the question of repression. Conservative and Labour governments alike spent the 70s grasping for means to contain both this rising militancy, and the spiralling political crisis gripping the country.

Successive anti-immigration laws in 1962, 1968 and 1971 were a potent weapon of state racism, granting the British increased control over the lives of non-white people in Britain. In the midst of 'The Troubles', Britain's protracted war in the North of Ireland, the Labour government introduced the Prevention of Terrorism Act in 1974. It was the first of a series of 'counter-terror' laws which would later be consolidated in the Terrorism Act 2000 and serve as the backbone of its unimaginably broad 'national security' apparatus to this day.

In 1968, the notorious 'Spycops'/Special Demonstration Squad division of the Met Police's Special Branch was formed in response to the rise of Black Power and the New Left – a division whose sordid exploits are being uncovered in an Undercover Police Inquiry which finally commenced its hearings in 2020.[17]

HN356/HN124 is the code attached to Spycop Billy Biggs, who infiltrated the Socialist Workers Party (SWP) branch in Brixton from 1978–81, even getting elected as their treasurer. Biggs was present in 1979 in Southall at the demonstration

17 To keep up to date with the inquiry, follow the *Police Spies Out of Lives* website on Spycops: https://spycops.co.uk.

against the National Front that saw the killing of Blair Peach by the Met's Special Patrol Group. He reported on the Anti-Nazi League, Right to Work Campaigns and the Campaign Against Racism and Fascism, and also likely on the Brixton Defence Campaign. Among his reports to Special Branch are: a leaflet advertising the Black Peoples Day of Action and meetings of the SWP, including an event entitled, 'From Riots to Revolution.' In 1981, towards the end of his undercover deployment, MI5 was particularly interested in the 'SWP's future direction, particularly as regards blacks'.[18]

Meanwhile, Britain's police didn't so much reveal their reactionary political character in this period – through their increasingly aggressive suppression of social unrest – as revel in it. Policing bodies took on an increasingly agitational, pressure group role in British politics – a tendency embodied by Sir Robert Mark, once described as 'perhaps the first real police ideologist'.[19] During his time as Deputy Commissioner and Commissioner of the Met Police between 1968–77, Mark inveighed against juries, the left, the Labour Party and the media, while redefining the role of the police chief as an explicitly political actor.[20]

In 1980, the St Pauls district of Bristol served a warning shot from Black youth reaching boiling point in the face of inces-

18 *Security Service Minute Sheet concerning requests for information on South London SWP groups*, Undercover Policing Reference UCPI0000028839, https://ucpi.org.uk/publications/security-service-minute-sheet-concerning-requests-for-information-on-south-london-swp-groups (last accessed August 2021).

19 Stephen Sedley, (1981). 'The Growing Police Challenge', *Marxism Today*, 25:4, (April 1981), accessed at: banmarchive.org.uk/collections/mt/index_frame.htm (last accessed August 2021).

20 For more on Robert Mark and the increased politicisation of police forces during this period, see Tony Bunyan's book, *The history and practice of the political police in Britain* (London: Quartet Books, 1983).

sant police harassment. The Black & White cafe, popular among local working-class residents, including Bristol's Black community, was targeted by police who harassed youths, carried out raids and assaulted residents. According to Avon & Somerset Police themselves, the Black & White Cafe has been raided more times than any building in the country. On 2 April 1980, Black & White reacted to the latest raid on the cafe by attacking police and destroying police vehicles. Over 100 would be arrested, with almost all charged – but none being convicted by a jury of their peers.

Bristol's show of strength foreshadowed the major urban uprisings a year later, and was immortalised by demonstrators in Brixton who led their charge against racist police with chants of 'Bristol yesterday, Brixton today'.

An uneven movement

Black Power in Britain was far from perfect or coherent as a movement.

Reflecting its youthful orientation, its organisations were uneven and fractious, and their communiques brusque, iconoclastic and at times perhaps overly masculinist – comparing the racism befalling Black men as a form of 'castration', and defining their role as defending the 'rape' of Africa by colonialism, for example.

Despite emphasising the importance of Black* women in struggle in theory, women were typically relegated within Black Power organisations, leading to the formation of women's caucuses and then separate Black women's organisations. These came together with the formation of OWAAD in 1978, who asserted their decision to self-organise in light of the failings of the conventional socialist, women's liberation and Black Power organisations to integrate their multiple oppressions:

> We cannot divorce our position as women from our historical and present-day experiences of racism. To concentrate on our oppression as women and ignore the State's many-sided attacks on Black people, would be to pretend that Britain is not a racist society. Similarly, we cannot divorce our experience as members of the (black) working class from the exploitation we experience as women.[21]

Fuelled in part by the inability of its members to address and integrate the question of women's sexuality into their work, OWAAD itself would unravel five years after launching.[22]

And finally, whether one attributed the blame for division to those Black Power organisations or to the patronising attitude of the 'white left', the rejection of collaboration with the white socialists saw some Black Power organisations slip into a wholesale rejection of class struggle as a motor of change, which stymied their potential for revolutionary transformation in Britain. But to identify these shortcomings is not to dismiss Black Power in Britain – any more than it would be to dismiss their much-storied counterparts in the US, who suffered many of the same problems. Given the time and the tools, nascent

21 'OWAAD Draft Constitution', (c.1978), DADZIE/1/1/2, *Stella Dadzie Papers*, held at: London: Black Cultural Archives.

22 For analyses on factors leading to OWAAD's collapse, see Nydia A. Swaby, 'Disparate in Voice, Sympathetic in Direction: Gendered Political Blackness and the Politics of Solidarity', *Feminist Review*, 108:1, (2014), pp. 11–25; Beverly Bryan, Stella Dadzie & Suzanne Scafe, *Heart of the Race Black Women's Lives in Britain* (London & New York: Verso, 2018), pp. 176–7; Brixton Black Women's Group. 'Black Women Organizing', *Feminist Review*, 17, (1984), pp. 84–9, https://libcom.org/library/black-women-organising-brixton-black-womens-group (last accessed August 2021).

Black Power organisations could have untangled the contradictions embedded within their movements and move towards a new dawn in Britain.

Tragically, they were never given the chance.

Chapter 3

1981 and the road to antiracism from above

By July 1981, the pollution from Bradford's famed textile mills no longer hung quite as thick as it once did. Rather, those days, it was replaced by the haze of fear suffocating the city air, a creeping anxiety lingering in the summer nights.

During the early years of Thatcher's first government, Black and brown communities were subject to rampant racist violence, menaced by far-right street forces across the country, which visited upon them frequent punishing attacks.

Whenever the fascists struck, African, Caribbean and Asian communities were wounded twice over – first at the hands of the racists, then at the cold indifference of the police.

Upon hearing rumours that Bradford was to be the next town targeted in the summer of 1981, some young locals from the United Black Youth League (UBYL) – a radical group splintered off from the Bradford Asian Youth Movement (AYM) – opted for active defence rather than appeals to apathetic authorities.

Drawing upon the tactical repertoire familiar for the time, they prepared milk bottles filled with petrol and rags to stave off any advances by skinheads, should they indeed strike. The march never materialised and the bottles were never used – but twelve Asian men, and briefly one woman, were arrested, with the men being charged with the offences of 'making an explosive' under the Explosive Substance Act 1881, and 'conspiracy to make explosive substances', under the Criminal Law Act 1977.

Echoing examples like the Mangrove Nine trial a decade earlier,[1] the trial of the Bradford 12 served as a legal watershed of activist-advocacy, and its defence campaign galvanised support across the country and across the world, from Guyana, Sri Lanka, Canada and Ireland. As the case stretched out into the next year, mass pickets and protests hundreds deep were organised for court dates, rallying around the powerful slogan: 'Self-defence is no offence'.

In summer 1982, the Bradford 12 stepped out of Bradford Crown Court as free men. Almost exactly 15 years later Marsha Singh, former chair of the Bradford AYM from which the UBYL had split, was swept into the House of Commons – as newly elected Labour MP for Bradford West. While evading the murky moral depths sunk to by his New Labour colleagues – Singh spoke out forcefully, even eloquently, against the Iraq War, to his credit – he broadly made peace with their programme, failing to counter their broader agenda as vigorously as some of his firebrand fellow lawmakers. As MP, he voted through the Labour government's repressive counterterror laws which, if in place a few decades earlier, would have almost certainly spelled a darker fate for his former comrades on trial.

When Bradford was indeed ablaze 20 years on from the affair of 1981 – with Asian youth reacting to violence and provocation from white racists – the question of 'self-defence' was by then far from Singh's concerns. Instead, his response to the Bradford riots was to pour scorn on the youth: denouncing the incident

1 The 1970 trial of nine Black activists, on the charge of incitement to riot at a demonstration against the Metropolitan police's harassment of the Mangrove restaurant in Notting Hill. The trial was significant for some of the defendants' decision to represent themselves in court, and for demanding to be heard before Black jurors.

as 'sheer criminality', even advocating the use of water cannons to quell the disturbances.[2]

Meanwhile, his maiden speech[3] in November 1997 was in many ways the epitome of moderation. Aside from a critique of India's brutal occupation of Kashmir – an issue dear to his Pakistani-Kashmiri constituents – and a dig at Bradford council, the speech was an affable induction into the formalities of political life. Rather than speaking on his city's proud history of struggle, Singh's new colleagues were treated to a milquetoast ode to multiculturalism. In place of the type of radical self-organisation that had once shaped his own politics was a tribute to the Labour Party that had secured him office. And instead of active communities of resistance, the people of Bradford were reduced to simple constituents: concerned citizens to be rhetorically summoned up and summarily discarded before his audience.

This stands as but one example of Antiracism from Above in action: through which radical antiracism was contained and incorporated into the mould of formal British politics, where gradualism and moderation prevailed, and where individual career trajectories substituted for social progress writ large.

The road to 1981

While Marsha Singh may not have deigned to mention it in his maiden speech, his presence in Parliament was indebted to

2 'We may look at European models of crime controls, seven hours in White Abbey Road could have been cleared in half an hour with a water cannon.' https://thetelegraphandargus.co.uk/news/8040086.amp (last accessed August 2021); https://thetelegraphandargus.co.uk/news/8040091.sheer-criminality-is-the-root-cause (last accessed August 2021).

3 M. Singh, *Public Accounts debate*, HC Deb, 20 November 1997, c491, available at https://www.theyworkforyou.com/debates/?id=1997-11-20a.491.0 (last accessed August 2021).

the likes of the Bradford 12. In many ways, 1981 made Singh's passage to Westminster possible – or to be more precise, it was made possible by the strategy of containment and incorporation that followed the historic rebellions of that year.

The road to 1981 was well worn by struggles that have been etched into the history of the country: the Mansfield Hosiery Strike 1972, Imperial Typewriters Strike 1974, Notting Hill Carnival 'Riots' 1976, Grunwick Strike 1976–8, Battle of Lewisham 1977, and, in a harbinger of things to come, the uprisings in Bristol's St Pauls district, 1980.

Their antiracism was organised along both the labour and social fronts – but as these struggles radicalised, they grew into a frontal challenge to the fraying political order. Indeed, in demonstrating how the post-war political arrangement was unable to absorb and incorporate the Black and brown working class on the same footing as their white counterparts, these struggles struck at the very heart of the political crisis engulfing Britain. Something had to give. It is for this reason that the antiracist struggles of this era are remembered; for the very fact that they were not discrete incidents, but moments of reckoning for the British left and test runs for the 'New Right', at a time when an old order was disintegrating.

The Grunwick strike, famously headed by South Asian women workers at a photo-processing factory in North West London, serves as a particularly potent example. Over the course of nearly two years the strike was catapulted from a local dispute over dignity and racism at work into a pitched battle of national notoriety. As well as drawing support from unions across the country, it provoked showdowns in Parliament between the Labour government and the new Leader of the Opposition: Margaret Thatcher. Meanwhile, the hard-right National Association for Freedom (NAFF) served as early shock troops for

Thatcherism during the strike, providing political reinforcement to the Grunwick factory's owners while organising lawfare attacks against the unions on their behalf. Despite ending in defeat for the strikers, Grunwick has earned its rightful place in the British historical imaginary, though at times stripped of its racialised and gendered dimensions when retold as a straightforward trade union issue.

This is a legacy complicated, though certainly not negated, by the critiques levelled by contemporaries for the strikers' shift away from the model used at Mansfield towards a more formal trade union mode of struggle. Seen by some as a means for the trade union movement to co-opt an antiracist movement from below, commentators such as the Race Today Collective were sharp in their appraisal: 'The [trade union strategy] that the Grunwick strike committee has accepted and worked hard upon is a denial of their own history. This has been its greatest weakness.'[4]

Like the other flashpoints of this decade, Grunwick was therefore not just a political novelty – irreducible as it so often is to 'strikers in saris', or to eloquent strike leader Jayaben Desai – but part of a long arc of the struggle for the streets, the shop floors and, in no uncertain terms, the soul of Britain.[5]

The various protagonists and set pieces assembled during the course of the Grunwick strike would feature in key roles during the Conservative Party's long rule over Britain from 1979. The framing of Grunwick as a breakdown of public order would pave

4 'Grunwick Strike The Bitter Lessons', *Race Today*, 9:7, (November/December 1977), p. 152, accessed at https://archive.leftove.rs/documents/ADBD/4 (last accessed August 2021).

5 For more on the political significance of Grunwick, see the *Working Class History* podcast episode on Grunwick, featuring Sujata Aurora and Amrit Wilson: https://workingclasshistory.com/2018/02/28/episode-1-the-grunwick-strike-1976.

the way for the intensified law and order politics underpinning Thatcherism, while the 'flying pickets' witnessed during the dispute would be outlawed by the Employment Act 1980. The Met Police's brutal Special Patrol Group, deployed at Grunwick for the first time in its history at a labour picket, would be central to the policing of the 1981 'riots' – while Lord Scarman, who authored a whitewash report into the 'rioting' in Brixton, also headed an inquiry into Grunwick in a failed attempt to reconcile the parties involved. The trade union forces that converged over Grunwick would be broken by Thatcher's war against the labour movement – culminating with the defeat of the striking miners in 1985, who had lent such full-blooded support to Grunwick. The private enterprise evangelicals that had provided political backbone to Grunwick's bosses would find their kingdom come under Thatcher's programme, while the militant antiracism reaching its crescendo during Grunwick would be canalised and professionalised over the course of the 80s.

But in 1979, the pathway to Britain's hard-right reconstruction was not guaranteed – a fact of which the government was keenly aware. A secret 'Review of potential for civil disturbance in 1981' surveying the potential threats and flashpoints occurring during 1981 was undertaken by the Home Office. Against the backdrop of industrial unrest, anti-nuclear weapons mobilisations, the St Paul's rebellion of 1980, activity of the emboldened far right and violence by Scottish and Welsh nationalists, the review concluded with the emphatic warning that 'violence in the ethnic minority communities is likely'.[6]

Unfortunately for the Home Office, they were textbook victims of bad timing: the review was published a mere two

6 'Civil disorder disturbances in Brixton, Bristol, Liverpool, Manchester and London districts', (1981) PREM 19/484, Records of the Prime Minister's Office: Correspondence and Papers, 1979–1997, held at: Kew: The National Archives.

weeks *after* the legendary Brixton uprisings against the police in April had already taken place.

A turning point

The year 1981 was the convergence point of racist law and order policing, a biting economic recession and skyrocketing unemployment, years of fascists terrorising communities, and the passage of the racist British Nationality Act 1981. It was both a high tide and a turning point in British antiracism, most often remembered for the uprisings in cities across the summer.

Yet it opened not with the defiant call to rebellion, but the piercing screams of panicked children. The night of 17–18 January took with it 13 young Black lives at a birthday party in South East London for Yvonne Ruddock and Angela Jackson: the New Cross Massacre.[7] Widely understood as the result of a racist firebombing – fitting in with a pattern in recent years of attacks against Black communities – the fire confirmed the worst fears of Black communities besieged by attacks and arson in Thatcher's Britain.

The tragedy was immediately precipitated by a statement two weeks prior by Conservative MP Jill Knight, member of the far-right Monday Club group, where she appeared to condone white vigilante action against West Indian parties. For the parents and peers of the killed, the pain of the incident was compounded first by the cruel intrigues of the investigating police – who tried to force out false confessions from fellow partygoers and

7 Details about the New Cross Massacre and the Black People's Day of Action used in this section are mostly drawn from the description in Robin Bunce and Paul Field's *Renegade: The Life and Times of Darcus Howe* (London: Bloomsbury, 2017); and John La Rose, Linton Kwesi Johnson and Gus John's *The New Cross Massacre Story Interviews with John La Rose* (London: Bloomsbury, 2020).

deny racist intent to the attack. Then by the calculated indifference of the government – who made no acknowledgement of the incident for over a month. These provoked a mass response from Black communities across Britain which would culminate in the Black People's Day of Action on 2 March.

With 20,000 demonstrators marching across London on a weekday, the Black People's Day of Action was a physical show of defiance against those that had long assailed Black Britain: the police, politicians and press. In the months leading in to the Day of Action the New Cross Massacre Action Committee (NCMAC), headed by seasoned organisers Darcus Howe and John La Rose, coordinated a fact-finding mission to outmanoeuvre police inaction, collected testimonies, assisted fundraising to support the grieving families, and tackled the official smokescreen of disinformation from the state and media.

In building for the demonstration, the NCMAC toured the country, tapping into the existing infrastructure of organisations while seeing off attempts at co-option from the likes of the local state Community Relations Committees. At a march to the site of the fire, attempts by some local leaders to turn it into an homage to the US Civil Rights movement with chants of 'We Shall Overcome' fell flat when the streets were occupied by most of the thousands in attendance. While often overshadowed by the heat and light of the uprisings later that year, the Black People's Day of Action was a zenith of Black self-organisation in Britain, a symbol of confidence for Black communities, and a watershed for Antiracism from Below.

Riots, repression and reorientation

Enraged by this show of defiance, the Metropolitan Police struck back for revenge just a month later. Under Operation 'Swamp

'81', saturation policing by uniformed and plain-clothed police officers in Brixton, Lambeth resulted in mass, indiscriminate stop and searches, during which 943 people were stopped over six days, over half of whom were Black. As Leila Hassan Howe retold in 2011: 'Everyone was talking about it in Brixton, you couldn't go anywhere without being stopped. It was overwhelming, the sheer numbers of police involved.'[8]

The name of the operation was itself steeped in racist signifiers – consciously echoing Thatcher's infamous statement on immigration from a 1978 interview, that 'people are really rather afraid that this country might be rather swamped by people with a different culture'. Tellingly, local community leaders were not informed of the operation in advance – in bypassing the traditional bulwarks of moderation, the police came up against the youth of Brixton, unrestrained.

It was on 10 April that the first anti-police rebellion broke out in Brixton, after a Black man who had been stabbed was seen being loaded into a police van, and over the course of three days in April, the people of Brixton were in pitched battles with the police forces that had rained misery upon them for years.

Brixton raised the siren in April. The call was heeded across the country by summer. That July, Brixton was joined by massive rebellions in Handsworth in Birmingham, Chapeltown in Leeds, Moss Side in Manchester, Hyson Green in Nottingham and Toxteth in Liverpool – during which police deployed paramilitary tactics to quell the upsurge. Smaller skirmishes broke out in dozens of cities across the country. In West London's Southall, mass antifascist clashes led by Asian youth saw the Hambrough tavern, host to a skinhead band, razed to the ground. In Bradford, the United Black Youth League prepared to defend

8 Bunce & Field, *Renegade*, p. 330.

their communities from fascists. Two weeks later the Bradford 12 were arrested.

The 1981 uprisings were a deep shock to the system for the British political class. Their response rested first and foremost on repression, but also on a strategic reorientation to contain the militancy simmering in communities across the country. It is through this that the ascendancy of modern Antiracism from Above was set in motion.

In January, New Cross burned without a word from the government. When Brixton was set ablaze in April, their wall of silence shattered. The first response of Thatcher's government gravitated, naturally, towards law and order. The role of the police in quelling the uprisings was regularly flaunted by the government, with internal briefings reserving special praise for the despised Special Patrol Group. Speaking in Parliament the day after the April Brixton rebellion, Home Secretary Willie Whitelaw began with a tribute to officers' 'great bravery and professionalism'[9] – meanwhile Thatcher's meetings with community leaders after the summer riots appeared, at times, more like attempts to pry out a statement of support for their local police.[10] Running on a law and order ticket, the local council elections in Lambeth the month after the uprisings saw a marked swing towards the Tories.

Odes to law and order were matched in deed. Following the riots, armaments and equipment were procured for the police from the Ministry of Defence – including water cannons, as well as rubber bullets and riot guns, battle tested in the North of

9 W. Whitelaw, *Brixton (Disturbances)*, HC Deb, 13 April 1981, c21, available at https://hansard.parliament.uk/Commons/1981-04-13/debates/3453d3d1-6997-4911-8044-4899a4bfc260/Brixton(Disturbances).

10 Records of the Prime Minister's Office, 'Civil disorder disturbances in Brixton, Bristol, Liverpool, Manchester and London'.

Ireland. Military camps were made available for prison overflow, while anti-rioting tactics were drawn from policing as deployed in the North of Ireland and colonial Hong Kong. The Cabinet placed serious consideration on introducing a new Riot Act to augment policing powers on demonstrations.

Many of the legacies of the policing of 1981 ripple through today. During the uprisings, CS Gas was used for the first time against demonstrators on the British mainland in Toxteth – having previously only been used across the Irish Sea to quash uprisings against the British occupation in the North of Ireland. In the Scotland Yard Review of the 2011 London Riots, entitled 'Four Days in August', CS Gas was considered as a tactic to be deployed more extensively in future unrest. A week before this recommendation was released, CS Gas was thrown into the car of Anthony Grainger when he was killed by police officers – during an operation that later was found to be riddled with errors on the part of Greater Manchester Police.[11]

Meanwhile in 1985, a paper by the Association of Chief Police Officers (ACPO) made several references to the 1981 riots, stating how they had demonstrated the need for a 'new approach to policing disorder.'[12] As the Special Branch Project said, this new approach has three specific outcomes worth noting. Firstly, the National Reporting Centre used in the 1972 Miners' Strike and in further industrial disputes was to be placed on a more permanent footing. New training procedures for 'inner city disorder' were created, and thirdly, the ACPO *Public Order*

11 https://theguardian.com/uk-news/2019/jul/11/anthony-grainger-inquiry-police-blame-fatal-shooting (last accessed August 2021).

12 Association of Chief Police Officers of England, Wales and Northern Ireland, *A Paper to the A.C.P.O. Council on policing arrangement of the National Union of Mineworkers Dispute 1984/85*, available at https://documentcloud.org/documents/5080929-1985-10-ACPO-Paper-to-ACPO-Council-on-Policing.html#document/p5/a487041 (last accessed August 2021).

Manual of Tactical Options, and Related Matters was created and disseminated across the force. This training and handbook would provide much of the backbone of the upcoming working-class rebellion against the state; the 1984–5 Miners' Strike.

Mass arrests and 'snatch squads' became a feature of the policing of 1981, with hundreds of people in Manchester arrested in relation to the uprising. In a 1992 BBC documentary, looking back at his time as Chief Constable of Greater Manchester, James Anderton summarised his strategy for the riots, 'When trouble arises and violence occurs on the street, you hit it fast and hard. And that's what we did.'[13]

Anderton was known by his peers as 'God's copper', believing the police to be a moral enforcer for his Christian faith, and he spent much of his time as constable concerned with the growing threat of trade unions and in particular the potential for left-wing mobilisations. Anderton's violent response to the uprisings gained attention and praise across the police and political establishment, with Willie Whitelaw describing it as a 'conspicuous success.' Anderton would later be protected by Thatcher after a series of public comments saying queer people and those dealing with addictions who had contracted AIDS were falling in a 'cesspit of their own making'[14] in 1986, and calling for the reintroduction of corporal punishment the year after, stating he would 'beat criminals himself until they begged for mercy'.[15] His frequent public outbursts would cost him the chance to be Commissioner of the Metropolitan Police, but his peers elected

13 *My Way*, BBC Documentary, 1992.

14 http://news.bbc.co.uk/1/hi/programmes/panorama/4348096.stm (last accessed August 2021).

15 Home Office stays Aloof over Anderton Outburst (1987). The Glasgow Herald. https://news.google.com/newspapers?id=6DhAAAAAIBAJ&sjid=LlkMAAAAIBAJ&pg=4272%2C4117597 (last accessed August 2021).

him President of the Association of Chief Police Officers and he would later receive a knighthood. This was just one of the characters setting the tone of the response to the riots.

But beyond ratcheting up repression, the government was forced to pivot towards securing greater consent from racialised communities after the riots too. Central to this was the commissioning of an inquiry days after the April Brixton uprisings, which was tasked with '[inquiring] urgently into the serious disorder in Brixton on 10–12 April 1981 and to report, with the power to make recommendations'. Lord Scarman, undeterred by his failure to affect change during his earlier inquiry into Grunwick, was charged with undertaking what would become known as the Scarman report.

Published a mere four months after the explosion of the summer uprisings, Scarman's report was decidedly tepid. It famously proclaimed that '"Institutional racism" does not exist in Britain: but racial disadvantage and its nasty associate racial discrimination, have not yet been eliminated'.[16] Scarman's mild criticisms of the police conduct in the lead up to Brixton only served as preamble to a report that gave them a firm stamp of approval – praising the police's behaviour during the riots, even accepting the need for elements like the Special Patrol Group and plastic bullets in the course of policing. The proposed reforms centred around developing a more consultative and collaborative approach between police and local communities, as well as better training and diverse recruitment for police forces. The government response to the report led to the expansion of community policing strategies that incorporated community organisations as joint stakeholders in policing.

---

16 Leslie Scarman, *The Scarman Report Brixton Disorders 10–12 April 1981* (Middlesex: Penguin, 1986), p. 209.

In the words of Kalbir Shukra, 'The question which Scarman addressed was not how to eradicate racism but how policing could be enforced without provoking further outbreaks of disorder.'[17] The outcomes of this strategy were uneven but clear – the police and political class were broadly able to contain the militant opposition to police abuse which still seethed below the surface.

Despite fierce local riots against police brutality in 1985, 1995 and 2001, they did not again reach the same national scale until summer 2011, when the streets of England were aflame after the police murder of Mark Duggan.

'They will not let us belong'

All the while, racism kept grinding on. Working-class racialised communities stayed locked in cycles of poverty, presided over by hawkish police forces which increasingly began to reflect their complexion. Their housing situations remained dire, while town halls and the House of Commons grew more diverse. Racial terror still stalked the land; contemporary publications on race attacks still read like a catalogue of horrors. A new far-right force emerged to pollute British politics anew, and the British National Party won their first elected councillor in 1993.

For all its limitations, the Antiracism from Above of the post-1981 years remained an approach that resonated powerfully with excluded communities in Britain. Interviewed for a piece in *Marxism Today* shortly after the anti-Rushdie demonstrations, a young Muslim in Bradford drew explicit comparisons between the action that they took and the trajectory for Black people after 1981: 'It is our Brixton . . . They took Afro-Caribbeans seri-

17 Kalbir Shukra, *The Changing Pattern of Black Politics in Britain* (London: Pluto, 1998) p. 115.

ously after the riots, didn't they? Well, now they're going to take us seriously.'[18]

In the years following the Rushdie affair, Muslim organisations engaged in a process that culminated with the formation of an umbrella organisation to represent them in making claims upon government. The Muslim Council of Britain (MCB) was formed in 1997 – the same year that saw the election of Britain's very first Muslim MP, Mohammed Sarwar, and a New Labour government that initially sought to position itself as a friend to marginalised communities. Those heady days certainly seemed to herald a new dawn for Muslim communities in Britain, akin to the advancements made in the post-1981 era.

But for others who had witnessed history from a different vantage point, the promise offered up by the future at the tail end of the 80s appeared dim. Also quoted in that same *Marxism Today* piece was a former member of the Bradford 12, his words aching with resentment: 'We live in this meaningless democracy and we are nothing. We do not belong, they will not let us belong. They think we are monkeys, not people. We should get out.'[19]

18 Yasmin Alibhai, 'A Member No More', *Marxism Today*, (December 1989), accessed at banmarchive.org.uk/collections/mt/index_frame.htm (last accessed August 2021).

19 Ibid.

Chapter 4

Antiracism as status quo

> The question the inner cities raise, therefore, is are we to become a successful, multi-racial nation or are we on a course for a revolutionary phase in our history? – Lord Scarman[1]

Scarman, Thatcherism and the Labour Party

The development of Antiracism from Above did little to relieve racialised communities of the stark injustices facing them, but it disarmed of the means in which to organise forcefully against them. The Scarman review was central to this process.

The government's adoption of Scarman's recommendations was patchy. They were happy with those advising policing innovations, but predictably dithered in tending to the general issue of social conditions – and the specific issue of 'racial disadvantage' – that Scarman pointed to as contributing factors in the uprisings. But beyond the implementation, or lack thereof, of specific recommendations, Scarman and the government found consensus on the need for a containment strategy, to control the problem of Britain's racialised communities in revolt. This lay in part through the ratcheting up of policing, but also in the task

1 Scarman, *The Scarman Report Brixton*, p. xiii.

of managing the movements that had set those communities in motion over the last decade and a half.

Ultimately Scarman formed one plank of a broader political reorientation towards racialised communities and towards antiracism. Post-Scarman developments played out along a dual strategy, whereby the central government ratcheted up repression while local Labour councils practised forms of co-option to canalise discontent away from spilling into the streets. This would quickly dovetail with the incorporation of Black* politics into the Labour Party, refashioned as the 'natural home of Black people'.

Steered in one direction by the right-wing Tory government, steered in another by left-led Labour councils, they came together as curious bedfellows to create a layer of antiracist activists and apparatchiks whose funding, employment and sometimes status were tethered to the machinery of the local and central state.

This was coupled with moves to draw racialised communities in to state apparatus such as the police – which was achieved through a mix of community-police partnerships, the development of 'community policing' models rather than the more overtly confrontational styles seen previously, and recruitment drives: the panacea of a multiracial police force that continues to be prescribed after every anti-police flare.

The development of Antiracism from Above was not simply a grand conspiracy hatched from the mind of Margaret Thatcher. Rather, it was the sum of many moving parts: initiatives and political experiments from central government, local governments, emerging disciplines within the academy and these tendencies already circulating within British antiracism. It was a mix of top-down and bottom-up pressures.

And crucially, these converged at a new historical conjuncture in Britain – one represented by the rise to power of the British New Right, and the release of raw anger in the summer of 1981. It was in this context that the tensions between the hard-right Tories and the left of the labour movement ended up being, in curious ways, complementary rather than contradictory. The realignment of politics under the Thatcher era forced a certain layer of antiracists into a closer alliance with sections of the Labour Party, which Black Power organisations had traditionally shunned. Meanwhile, experiments in 'municipal socialism' by the Labour Party's left in major cities opened up spaces for the absorption of antiracist organising into the fold of formal politics in a way which wasn't previously possible.

Mechanics of multiculturalism

Antiracism from Above found its ideological expression in the doctrine of state multiculturalism, which reached its high point with the election of the New Labour government in 1997.

While its roots stretched back to the immediate post-war years, British state multiculturalism emerged in its contemporary form through the 1970s, once the division of (white) natives and (non-white) foreigners was no longer simple and clean, and a new social mechanism of integration for non-white people was needed.

This shift was catalysed by the official response to 1981, where Scarman's report reflected a liberal multiculturalist ethos – for example, by stating that 'training of police officers must prepare them for policing a multi-racial society'.[2] Multiculturalism also undergirded the policy of GLC and left Labour councils in the

2 Scarman, *The Scarman Report Brixton*, p. 126.

80s, which shaped the character of its antiracist programmes. To be sure, the development of state multiculturalism was not seamless. Scarman's proposals around social change grated against the Conservative government's unbridled racism, and the emphasis on antiracism, feminism and gay rights by the Labour left served as an attack point for the Conservative government and Labour right-wingers, against what they caricatured as the 'Loony Left'.

Ultimately, however, multiculturalism won the day, and over the decades Antiracism from Above was codified in the doctrine of state multiculturalism – where a nominally antiracist politics was allotted a corner in the political landscape. There, professional antiracists were able to stake out a presence in mainstream British politics, as pundits and talking heads, as long as they did not bring into question the underlying political status quo. This arrangement reached its apex as part of the governing ideology of the New Labour governments, before the 2007/08 financial crash led to the decline of state multiculturalism.

In this way, Antiracism from Above became entangled with the British state rather than presenting an opposition to it. Multiculturalism served as a means for the state to manage the contradictions of governing a racist society without meaningfully addressing them – instead enveloping them in a dense vocabulary of 'culture', 'ethnicity', 'diversity', 'identity' and so on.

At worst, multiculturalism provided an alibi for racist state agencies. This contradiction was laid bare in a pamphlet by the National Convention of Black Teachers on policing and race training, highlighting how between 1981–4:

> [The] police training establishment implemented a number of new programmes. So that cadets, recruits and officers may now be taught multi-agency policing methods in the morning

> and commando work in the afternoon: multiculturalism in one course and the use of plastic bullets in the next: concepts of American-imported racism-awareness on the one hand and Northern Ireland style repression on the other.[3]

As multiculturalism was elevated to an ideology of governance, racism itself was emptied of its ideological substance. This was underlined by the response to policing following the 1981 uprisings, whereby the question of state racism which the police were *enforcing* became recast as a matter of racial attitudes *among* the police. More broadly, structural racism was refashioned as an issue of *managing* racist attitudes and interpersonal hostility. This in turn held the door open for apolitical and procedural 'solutions' to racism – such as the new Racism Awareness Trainings prescribed by professional antiracists.

After the 1981 uprisings, such professionals were drawn from the ranks of organisations like RAPU (Racism Awareness Programme Unit) to help in smoothing out the hard edges of the police force. Nearly 40 years later, their US counterparts were soothing the hearts of white America, as Robin DiAngelo's *White Fragility* shot to the top of bestseller lists at the height of the 2020 Black Lives Matter protests. Labour leader Keir Starmer's warmest gesture towards the protests was to prescribe 'unconscious bias training' for his MPs. And before the dust had settled, race consultants on both sides of the Atlantic were polishing up their portfolios and waxing lyrical about their 'anti-oppression workshops' and 'antiracist dinner parties', like shameless antiracist ambulance chasers.

---

3 National Convention of Black Teachers, *Police Racism and Union Collusion – the John Fernandes Case*, (n.d.), p. 9, accessed at: http://ucu-retired-london.org.uk/police-racism-and-union-collusion-the-john-fernandes-case (last accessed August 2021).

This emphasis on racism as a procedural matter continued to be reflected in, for example, the Macpherson definition of 'institutional racism' following the Stephen Lawrence inquiry in 1999, which defined the term as referring to: 'The collective failure of an organisation to provide an appropriate and professional service to people because of their colour, culture, or ethnic origin [which can] be seen or detected in *processes, attitudes and behaviour*'[4] (emphasis added). And importantly, the watershed Macpherson report still only found institutional racism *in* the Metropolitan Police Force, rather than identifying them *as* the organised expression of state racism.

Such a mechanical understanding of racism necessarily reshapes antiracist action: if racism is a matter of procedure, then antiracism doesn't require mass struggle, but rather for pressure to be exerted on the levers of institutional power to enforce antiracist policies. State multiculturalism also provided the opportunity to drown out the sensibilities of radical Black* politics that had developed in the era of Black Power.

All movements for justice are fraught with contradictions. This much will be clear to anyone who has engaged in organising, and found themselves forced to struggle over political lines and clarity within their organisations almost as fiercely as they must with wider society. This is as much the case in antiracism as in another other field of organising, and the Black Power era was no exception.

Reflecting on the demise of UCPA, founder Obi Egbuna spoke on the disparate ways in which members understood the purpose of the organisation, and how this fractured UCPA from within:

---

4 *The Stephen Lawrence Inquiry* https://assets.publishing.service.gov.uk/government/uploads/system/uploads/attachment_data/file/277111/4262.pdf, p. 49 (last accessed August 2021).

> Within [UCPA], there were members who believed that the answer to the black man's problem lay in the overthrow of the capitalist system, and there were others who felt it lay in the Black man going to the House of Lords; there were some who saw themselves as part of the international Black revolution, and there was a faction who believed that the Black man in this country should concern himself only with what goes on in this country... in short, it became all too clear that what we had was not one movement, but movements within a movement.[5]

Though UCPA emerged as Black Power in Britain was in its infancy, these contradictions never went away. Rather, these various ideological tendencies were strengthened or silenced at any given time either by internal motion of Black Power politics, or the external pressures applied by the state. By the early 1980s these contradictions had matured. What the development of Antiracism from Above did was to seize upon these already-existing conflicts, with multiculturalism empowering those tendencies who would have felt that the answer indeed lay in sending a Black man to the House of Lords.

Black* enterprise and the class question

> The British state finds it necessary . . . to create a black intermediary class to stand between the black working class and to collaborate with the state against the . . . radical and revolutionary struggles of the black working class and unemployed.

5 https://pasttenseblog.wordpress.com/2021/04/09/in-the-shadow-of-the-spg-racist-policing-resistance-black-power-in-1970s-brixton (last accessed August 2021).

> There is a titanic battle which is being waged between these two perspectives in the black community.[6] – John La Rose, 1983

> In other words, we must create a black British middle class. This was the strategy pursued in America. As in America, so here: black and brown as well as white faces must be seen not only on the production line but also in positions of authority and influence at all levels of society – Lord Scarman, 1986.

To succeed, the consolidation of Antiracism from Above had to deal with the question of the Black and brown working class, and lumpen elements – that stratum of society which responded to earlier attempts at co-option with Black Power, and shot across the bow of British politics through the 1970s. Not willing to settle for second-class status, not able to be bought off – in large enough numbers – by the machinery of the Community Relations Commission, and not possible to absorb within the post-war social compact, this was the social fraction that needed to be managed to ensure a smoother passage ahead for the government in the new decade.

Organisers at the time such as John La Rose, quoted above, were clear on what they understood the strategy of the government to be for Black communities. Firstly, it was to develop an intermediary layer between the state and working class, and secondly, expanding the ranks of the Black and brown 'middle class'. This would find ideological expression in the drive for entrepreneurialism under Thatcherism, and organisational expression in representation politics, covered below. The outcome was a new layer of Blacks and Asians that were middle class in aspiration, immodest in ambition, and moderate

6 John La Rose, Linton Kwesi Johnson, & Gus John, *The New Cross Massacre Story Interviews with John La Rose* (London: George Padmore Institute, 2020) p. 38.

in orientation – and who would form the new leading edge of antiracism in Britain.

Entrepreneurialism was a central feature of the Thatcherite project of remaking Britain; breaking the hegemony of 'old money' among the ruling class, creating opportunities for certain individuals to ascend up the social ladder, and developing a cultural agenda around 'bootstrap' self-sufficiency that disavowed the social collectivism of previous eras. Though the presence of Black and Asian capitalists in Britain was not itself novel – Grunwick owner George Ward was himself of Indian descent, for example – the capture of Blacks and Asians into this entrepreneurial project would have a predictably debilitating effect on antiracist political culture more broadly. As the logic of entrepreneurialism goes, the bleak indeterminacies of the future could be overcome by dealing with the inadequacies of the individual; recasting the do-it-yourself ethos of the Black Power era with a do-for-self ethic of individualism. Today this lives on in the perverse affection for Black or brown capitalism, and the myth that 'buying Black' is in itself a solution to the political problem of racism.

We can contrast this with the ethos professed by the likes of the Manchester Black Women's Co-op co-founded in 1974. While being sober about the fact that they 'do not expect the co-operative to solve the world's problems, or even all of our own', the Co-op's Preamble includes the ambition that through the co-op:

> [We] hope to replace: –
> 1. Dependence with *self-reliance*
> 2. Rivalry with *co-operation*
> 3. Individualism with *collective effort*

4. Striving for individual status with striving for collective excellence
5. Shame in ourselves with pride in our people's achievements
6. Defeatism, with confidence in the people's achievements
7. Indifference to the African revolution, with *firm support for our sisters and brothers who are struggling to free themselves and us* (emphasis added)[7]

One would be hard pressed to find today's ethnic enterprises espousing vocal support for (armed) revolutionary struggles in the Global South – or certainly not without engaging in the most cynical form of market gimmickry.

The expansion of the Black and Asian petit bourgeoisie and 'middle class', while remaining small, would also transform the shape of Black* politics. The deepening of class stratification among these communities contributed to the fragmentation of community politics, by forming a subsection of the community with materially different interests from the dispossessed masses. It also empowered the more self-serving tendencies present within those communities to claim more of the political agenda, and by the end of the 80s there was a fraction of the population which could speak of middle-class Blacks as '[having] done extraordinarily well' under Thatcher.[8]

By 1983, the Black Unity and Freedom Party analysed the emergence of a Black* petit bourgeoisie asserting itself as a movement, and how this differed from the presence of middle-class Blacks within the movement previously:

---

7 'Manchester Black Women's Forum', (c.1975), WONG/6/20, *Papers of Ansel Wong*, held at: London: Black Cultural Archives.

8 John Pitts, 'To Be Young, British and Black', *Black Enterprise*, (December 1989), pp. 86–98, accessed at: https://books.google.co.uk/books?id=sV4EAAAAMBAJ (last accessed August 2021).

> At that time [the mid '60s] the movement had not evolved sufficiently to make class differences clear and in fact there was a community of interests between the very small Peti Bourgeois [sic] and the rest of our community . . . With the passage of time we believe this community of interest now no longer holds.[9]

What was significant was less the fact of the existence of this petit bourgeois layer of Blacks and Asians, and more the fact that they were now able to advance their interests as the antiracist mainstream.

Under Thatcher's leadership, the Conservative Party even established two bodies towards which they would try and funnel this burgeoning constituency of enterprising nouveau riche ethnics – the Anglo Asian Conservative Society (AACS) and the National Anglo West Indian Conservative Society (NAWICS). It also appeared to take some leads from the American example. During his 1968 Presidential run and over the course of his term in office, Richard Nixon made an explicit attempt to redefine Black Power in the US into Black capitalism. While this project of building Black 'economic self-determination' was of mixed success on its own terms, it served to contain and break up the radical potential of Black Power which had shaken the nation in the years prior.

While the nominally 'raceblind' ethos of Thatcher's entrepreneurial project prevented such an overt appeal on her part in the UK, lessons from Nixon's Black capitalism permeated the government's response to the 1981 rebellions. This is evident both from the many references to the US example in the Scarman

9 'The Black Peti Bourgeois', *Black Voice*, 14:1, (1983), accessed at https://woodsmokeblog.files.wordpress.com/2017/10/1983-bufp-peti-bourgeois.pdf (last accessed August 2021).

report, as well as from declassified archival documents from the Prime Minister's Office during Thatcher's term. Buried near the end of a lengthy document around the riots is a report from Aylesbury MP and government minister, Timothy Raison, based on a recent trip to the US. Submitted to the Prime Minister in October 1981, the report recorded Raison's analysis on the development of race relations since the 1968 Black uprisings in America.[10] Alongside the stand-out success of 'getting blacks and other minorities on the economic ladder' Raison's report noted, tellingly, how Black business owners in the US 'accept that they will face problems but [seem] more prepared to try and overcome them with their own efforts rather than expect government to provide the solutions'.[11]

The report also emphasised the importance of helping 'facilitate organisations' that could operate within and on behalf of racialised communities, thereby allowing them to communicate certain ideals to their communities with a frankness unbecoming of government. The report also spoke on the value of propping up 'responsible black leaders' to function as intermediaries with black communities, as was by then the norm in the US – echoing Scarman's desire for a Black middle-class leadership who could 'exercise responsible and creative leadership in its own community and in the nation – to the benefit of all of us in Britain'.[12] Two days before the release of the Scarman report, Raison called the Prime Minister to advise her on overtures she could make to Black* communities in light of it.

10 'Civil disorder disturbances in Brixton, Bristol, Liverpool, Manchester and London districts', (1981) PREM 19/484. Records of the Prime Minister's Office: Correspondence and Papers, 1979–1997, held at: Kew: The National Archives.

11 Ibid.

12 Leslie Scarman, *The Scarman Report Brixton Disorders 10-12 April 1981* (Middlesex: Penguin, 1986), pp. xvi–xvii.

For its part, the Scarman report pinpointed the need for encouraging 'Black people to secure a real stake in their own community, through business and the progressions . . . if future social stability is to be secured'.[13] The government's response to this was to set up a number of initiatives to support small ethnic business including an 'ethnic minority business initiative' as well as training programmes. Internal government correspondence tracking the follow up to the Scarman report stressed that the Department of Employment 'does recognise that the ethnic minority groups represent a vast untapped source of entrepreneurial talent'.[14] Further initiatives in this vein were floated by Cabinet members, but ultimately in vain. Political divisions within the government sunk the plans, while racism still proved a compelling ideological pull: future Tory MPs Oliver Letwin and Hartley Booth infamously argued against targeted enterprise funding after the 1985 rebellions on the basis that doing so would merely 'subsidise Rastafarian arts and crafts workshops' and that these 'new entrepreneurs will set up in the disco and drug trade'.[15]

Thatcherism would certainly not liberate the toiling masses of Britain out of poverty; Black, brown or white. But promoting the ethos and possibilities of enterprise would help insulate the government from the full fury of working-class discontent.

The politics of recognition

Britain had long exploited the labour of racialised people, and the new entrepreneurial agenda had given some of them the

13 Ibid., pp. 167–8.

14 'HOME AFFAIRS. Civil disorder: Scarman Report on the 1981 Brixton riots; part 2', PREM 19/1521, Records of the Prime Minister's Office: Correspondence and Papers, 1979–1997, held at: Kew: The National Archive.

15 www.theguardian.com/politics/2015/dec/30/oliver-letwin-blocked-help-for-black-youth-after-1985-riots (last accessed August 2021).

opportunity to become exploiters themselves. But ultimately, Antiracism from Above would flounder as a project if it did not offer racialised communities some means of political expression, too.

The logic of what we term the 'politics of recognition' is simple, and seemingly intuitive. To be 'recognised' as a unit or constituency by the state, by its institutions – and, increasingly, by forces of the market – enables a turn towards civic politics. This allows one to mobilise claims upon the state, seek appropriate provisions from it and strive to become reflected within its institutions. The politics of recognition are a central pillar of Antiracism from Above and its strategy of inclusion – they are the cornerstone of a civil rights agenda, the means through which the sphere of legal rights available to individuals is expanded. And ultimately, it is the way in which racialised communities are formally incorporated into the British body politic.

But this civic turn is bound up in its own contradictions which mutually reinforce one another in a downward spiral. It is governed by a set of depoliticising forces that narrow the boundaries of antiracist politics. The forms of civic antiracism that have prevailed serve to shift the centre of gravity of political mobilisation towards representation politics which, at its lowest ebb, devolves into a deeply cynical form of tokenism; that of Black and brown faces in high places.

Essentially, it is a type of politics that prefers to silence political differences. Rather than the type of messy conflicts and contradictory political struggles that defined the life of the UCPA and countless others, figureheads of the politics of recognition prefer to build a project out of inert and uncomplicated demographic units – or constituencies – that they can speak on behalf of. In this way they can present themselves as brokers between government and 'the Black community', 'the Asian community' or 'the Muslim community', while in fact speaking to the desires of a very select layer of those communities. The process of transforming fluid communities into these flat demographic units often leads to those populations becoming frozen into static ethnic blocs, rather than flowering as radical political communities – cue endless debates about exactly who is part of this community, or where the ethnic boundaries lie in determining it. This *ethnic bloc politics* in turn reorganises community organising around itself, often degenerating into vote bank politics for one party or the next.

And finally, even once recognition has been granted to a group in policy or in law, social acceptance is always fragile and contingent. It is this that underlines anxieties about the supposed 'integration' or lack thereof of racialised communities in Britain, even those born in Britain. In the pursuit of maintaining acceptance, advocates of the politics of recognition often pander to respectability by uplifting the most socially 'valuable' or 'successful' examples – the industrious Muslim, the entrepreneurial immigrant – and often legitimise distinctions based on citizenhood and immigration status; between citizens who have a right to make claims upon the state, and non-citizens or 'illegals' who do not. Racialised communities in Britain had long been the object of political enmity, yet never been allowed to assert themselves as agents within the mainstream political landscape. They could hardly be blamed for seeking the politics of recognition as a path towards political self-determination, and by pooling their resources to craft a common agenda.

But ultimately, those who gained the most from this process were the figureheads and power brokers who could make their name on the backs of their communities' pain.

The Black sections

In the years following 1981, antiracist organisers took the path pioneered by the Grunwick strikers in the previous decade, and began to self-organise formally within the Trade Union movement, the Labour Party and more – rather than outside them, as per the Mansfield strike model. By way of initiatives like the Black Trade Unionists Solidarity Movement (BTUSM), set up in December 1981, they increased non-white representation of TU officials, and through groupings like Black Sections of the Labour Party, they increasingly joined the ranks of local, and then national politicians. Following Scarman's recommendations of diversifying the police force, Black and Asian police recruitment had also increased by 88% by July 1985.[16] Through the process of incorporation made possible by the opening of 1981, racialised people were gradually included into those very institutions that antiracist groups had confronted prior to 1981: for better or for worse.

The establishment of the Labour Party Black Sections (LPBS) by Labour Party activists in 1983 is emblematic of this shift. The Black Sections followed in the tradition of women's and youth caucuses within the party; self-organised spaces for Black* people to develop a common agenda, agitate for their representation in elected and leadership roles within the party – and effectively to get the Labour Party to better reflect the communities that loyally lent them their support. While the Black Sections never achieved their ultimate goal of being constitutionally recognised by the Labour Party, local Black Sections proliferated across the country, driving a significant increase in local political representation, and culminating with the election of four Black and

16 Records of the Prime Minister's Office, 'HOME AFFAIRS. Civil disorder: Scarman Report'.

Asian Labour MPs at the 1987 General Election: Diane Abbott, Paul Boateng, Bernie Grant and Keith Vaz.

Today, the LPBS are retrospectively recast by activists as the apogee of that phase of antiracist struggle; as the coming-of-age of the Black Power era. Yet contemporary debates on them cast a different light. What is well known is that the Black Sections faced bitter intransigence from the right by the Party's leadership – determined not to allow any show of strength from Black* people within the party, lest they lose support from racists among the electorate. But less remembered is the fact that numerous antiracist radicals of the time critiqued them from the left – pinpointing Black Sections less as a high tide of Britain's Black Power, and more the beginning of the end.

The milieu around *Race Today* and the Institute of Race Relations pointed to the growth of Black Sections as extraneous to the history of Black* working-class struggle, rather than a natural extension of it. And aside from this, critiques circulating on the edges of the British left had long underlined that the basic essence of the Labour Party was to decouple and corporatise class struggle away from the grassroots, rather than allow for the kind of synergy between community and party organising that Black Sections proponents sought.

In a 1985 interview with the Campaign Against Racism and Fascism, Sivanandan highlighted how the development of the LPBS should be seen in the context of a deepening class stratification among Black* communities: 'There is no such thing as a black-qua-black movement any more. There are middle-class blacks fighting for a place in the (white) middle-class sun and there are workless and working-class blacks fighting for survival and basic freedoms'.[17] John La Rose assessed the Black Sections

17 'UK commentary: Blacks & the Black Sections', *Race & Class*, 27:2, (1985), pp. 72–4.

similarly, saying that '[It] should be clear by now that a new period of the history, politics and perspective of this new black social grouping within the general middle classes in British society has begun'.[18]

For their part, members of the Black Sections national leadership were conscious of the accusations levelled against them, and towards the latter half of the 80s some of them did appear to grapple sincerely with the issue. In a March 1987 committee report, for example, co-founder/then-chair Marc Wardsworth conceded that there was a disconnect between the Black Sections and grassroots Black* working-class struggle, and that: 'There has been a tendency to go for short-term gains in selections and elections rather than the less-tangible long-term gains that persistent community-based work would bring'.[19] Another internal document from June 1987 stated that in order to avoid the LPBS 'becoming atrophied through organisational paralysis and a wide-spread perception that its 'careerist' leaders were 'cutting and running' into elective office', they would need to 'extend the frontiers of [their] struggle outside the party and into the Black communities'.[20]

Once the animating objective of electing Black and Asian MPs was in sight with the 1987 election, the question of how to develop a meaningful presence and engagement with grassroots Black* campaigns – rather than becoming immobilised by internal party politicking – became ever more pressing, leading

18 John La Rose, *Unending Journey selected writings* (London: New Beacon Books/ George Padmore Institute, 2014), p. 43.

19 'National Committee Report March 1987 – Going on the offensive with the Black Agenda', (March 1987), BG/P/11/5/2 (Pt 2), Labour Party Black Sections, held at London: Bishopsgate Institute.

20 'Campaign Black Links – The Way Ahead for Black Sections', (June 1987), BG/P/11/5/2 (Pt 2), Labour Party Black Sections, held at London: Bishopsgate Institute.

to a membership consultation and the development of the LPBS 'Black Agenda'.[21] Unfortunately for them, their ambitions to expand beyond the Labour Party came just as the noose tightened around them within the party. Chastened by attacks from the Labour Party leadership, the retreat of their left-wing allies within the party and the decline of the British left more broadly, the Black Sections wound up in the early 1990s. Its successor, the Black Socialist Society, managed to receive official affiliation to the party, albeit shorn of its element of self-organisation. This set the tone for the times – where representation became progressively decoupled from the idea of self-organisation in the mass sense, in favour of narrow visibility.

The gains made in the electoral arena by the LPBS during its lifetime were themselves mixed. Paul Boateng, who had made his name in the 70s and 80s as a firebrand challenging police violence, went on to fervently support draconian anti-terror policing, tougher asylum restrictions and the criminalisation of Eastern European beggars under the New Labour governments in which he served. While beginning his Parliamentary career with the bold rebuff to South African apartheid, 'Today Brent South, tomorrow Soweto!', Boateng soon joined pre-eminent apologists of Israeli apartheid, Labour Friends of Israel, as well as the board of mercenary company Aegis Defence Services – whose base of operations span Africa and the Middle East. After a string of scandals, and having long captured the Black Sections' distant successor body, BAME Labour, as his private fiefdom, Keith Vaz retired from Parliament in 2019 in disgrace. Diane Abbott has remained a stalwart of the Labour left, and the late Bernie Grant still holds a place in the heart of many

21 'Building for the 1990s' report (July 1989), BG/P/11/5/5, Labour Party Black Sections, held at London: Bishopsgate Institute.

antiracists – while his successor David Lammy has served as a model torchbearer of moderation.

The Black Sections and their ilk rode in on the crest of mass revolt, at a time when grassroots organising appeared to be in a phase of advance. As the tide began to ebb over the long years of struggle, signs of decay began to surface. As early as 1982, government correspondence was praising 'the more responsible black leaders [who] supported the police action' against a disturbance in Brixton as 'a new and most welcome development'[22] – echoing Timothy Raison's report.

When rebellions sparked off in Brixton 1995 in response to the police killing of Wayne Douglas, the disconnect between the new layer of Black officials and their communities had already become pronounced. These rebellions were contained much more swiftly, particularly through the moderating role played by Black political leaders in community policing arrangements established after Brixton 1981.

Upon the rise of the New Labour government by the tail end of the 90s, Kalbir Shukra contended that this difference had hardened into a sharp class antagonism, and that 'What began as a fracture between working-class black people and black public sector professionals [has] become a distinct conflict of interests between a layer of middle-class black people who have a stake in the system . . . and the majority of the ethnic minority population in Britain.'[23]

For as long as the demand of the Black Sections articulated themselves against the prevailing wisdom of white-dominated

22 'Civil disorder disturbances in Brixton, Bristol, Liverpool, Manchester and London districts', (1981) PREM 19/484, Records of the Prime Minister's Office: Correspondence and Papers, 1979–1997, held at: Kew: The National Archives.

23 Kalbir Shukra, *The Changing Pattern of Black Politics in Britain* (London: Pluto, 1998), p. 120.

society, they maintained a somewhat progressive sheen. But demands centred on representation in absence of a broader political programme are always ripe for co-option, and find their subversive qualities quickly negated. The fact that the Black Sections did begin to outline a proper political position until as late as 1987 certainly would not have helped them fend off claims of empty opportunism, or dampen accusations that they were pretenders to the cause of Black Power.

By the 25th anniversary of the Black Sections, Marc Wadsworth, while remaining broadly positive about their impact, conceded that although 'the Black Sections managed to get "black faces in high places", the movement itself was destroyed from within by the machinations of an unforgiving Labour Party and some short-sighted opportunists'.[24]

These were the fruits that came to bear in the 2021 London mayoral election.

This time the contest for Britain's capital, and political nerve centre, was headed by Labour's incumbent Sadiq Khan – of Pakistani background – against the Conservative Party's Shaun Bailey – of Jamaican heritage.

For all the symbolic gravity that could be imputed into this contest, one thing that stood out as clear was the relation of both the candidates to their respective ethnic 'communities'. Khan had spent his previous five years in position straining to put distance between him and his 'community' in order to appear as the model liberal leader for London. Meanwhile Bailey's history as a Tory Party devotee was, predictably, peppered with outbursts of prejudice and disrespect towards Black people and the

24 https://theguardian.com/commentisfree/2008/oct/06/race.labour (last accessed August 2021).

working class, many of which came back to haunt him on the election trail.[25]

Representing perhaps the apex of British representation politics thus far, the offer for London's electorate was an apathy-inducing ensemble. The incumbent served up a steadfast defence of a crushing status quo. His primary opponent offered deeply unpleasant platitudes from a British right wing nourished by the most noxious brand of nostalgia. For the poor and dispossessed of London, the promise of the next four years was clear: whether the future was brown or Black, their future looked bleak. This election was a prime example of the hollowness of representation politics, which takes up disproportionate space on mainstream antiracist agenda today – whether in terms of electoral politics, media, entertainment or beyond.

The subsidised revolution

The final pillar of Antiracism from Above in the post-1981 moment was the proliferation of a Black* civil society, often as part of a new race relations industry. In addition to special interest groups such as the BTUSM, this new civil society comprising a range of voluntary, third-sector and non-profit organisations began to emerge – often funded by local councils or the national Urban Aid programme – to support Black and brown communities through service provision or advocacy.

In and of itself, a professionalised or state-funded form of antiracist organising wasn't unique to the post-1981 moment: the United Black Youth League of the Bradford 12 had itself earlier split off from the Bradford Asian Youth Movement once the latter embarked down the path of state funding. The locali-

25 https://mirror.co.uk/news/politics/7-shocking-things-shaun-bailey-13389639 (last accessed August 2021).

ties that birthed the likes of the Black Panther Movement were awash with Urban Aid-funded projects by the early 70s, which served as the other side of the coin to state repression.

But after 1981, the Conservative Party was compelled to restart Urban Aid funding for programmes as well as refrain from plans to scrap the Commission for Racial Equality – going against their own ideological inclinations and retreating to the patterns of co-option tried by earlier governments. The impact of this Black* civil society lies not simply in the work it did, then, but how it transformed the character of antiracist organising. The work that these new organisations carried out had once been undertaken by radical groups – or independent projects connected to such groups – as part of a broader political project of serving Black and brown communities. Operating on an ethos of self-help and self-organisation, these independent organisations were central to the formation of radical communities, as discussed in Chapter 5.

Civil society organisations attempt to stand in for mass-based organisations and social movements by including some veneer of grassroots presence. But ultimately for the NGO or non-profit, the aim is to catch the ear of policymakers or the eyes of the media, rather than capture the hearts and minds of the masses. Individuals and communities often remain inert in this process, or merely used insofar as they can drum up appropriate coverage for a particular campaign.

There is, of course, a sliding scale when it comes to civil society – from plucky little organisations wrestling for survival each financial year, to large and thoroughly corporatised international outfits like Oxfam – and the interactions between different organisations and state power differs. But on the whole, civil society organising, as much in the 1980s as now, serves as a lid on grassroots organising. It does so by buying activists off the street and into advocacy roles, tying them down to the strictures of funding conditions and charity laws, and reproducing a division of organising work that is shaped more by the dictates of corporate management than movement development. And by making them accountable to funders and patrons, over the communities they seek to serve, these organisations end up forming a layer of professional activists sealed off from a popular base that prevents the formation of radical organisations.[26] Groups whose work would have once been driven by the democratic wills of their communities become dictated by the demands of funders, and open conflict with local and state politics grew muted as they played the fraught balancing act between seeking resources from that which they were critiquing. The political work of serving the people was subtly transformed into the task of service provision. One-time comrades came to be seen as competitors for funding pots. In this way any possible antiracist political movement is segmented both internally, and hived off from other grassroots movements externally, preventing the consolidation of a bloc that could meaningfully challenge political power, and retreating to legalistic strategies over mass organising.

At first glance, civil society-based antiracism appears to evade the pitfalls that befell the likes of the LPBS or Black enterprise – because they operate in a third space outside the private sector and electoral area. Yet the reality is that the new Black* civil society found itself enmeshed in the same ecosystem as the private and political sectors; on one hand drawing

26 To identify this is not, of course, to impugn every individual non-profit worker. Civil society organising often draws in activists with the noblest of intentions seeking to translate grassroots organising experience into advocacy, with the added reassurance of a pay cheque. It just as often churns them back out, thoroughly disgruntled and disillusioned.

on political patronage to secure funding streams to continue their work, on the other reproducing a form of entrepreneurial advocacy through professional antiracists. At the same time, under the neoliberal doctrine ushered in by Thatcherism, the very communities that these organisers and organisations were embedded in were decomposed by deindustrialisation and scattered by the winds of social decay. Arguably, in the broader sense it was this very 'third space' between business and politics that nurtured the cadres of New Labour's Third Way. These organisational networks formed the arteries of its equalities agenda, while serving as a conveyor belt for aspiring Labour politicians. This space was also where the (renewed) race relations industry flourished after 1981.

In her 1998 study of Black and Asian women organisations in Britain, Julia Sudbury challenged the notion of a straight line between funding for these new voluntary organisations and co-option. Instead, she presents a more intimate analysis of the way individual organisations navigated, subverted and resisted the challenges posed by funding,[27] as well as noting the different strategies adopted by the likes of the left-wing GLC, as opposed to more hostile councils elsewhere. When analysing specific organisations or localities, this is a fact certainly worth grappling with – but this does not negate the overall effect of the absorption into a Black* civil society. In their seminal text, *Heart of the Race*, Beverley Bryan, Stella Dadzie and Suzanne Scafe both take into account these complex tensions of having to defend control over funding, while firmly underscoring the overall effects of this 'subsidised revolution':

---

27 Julia Sudbury, *Other Kinds of Dreams: Black Women's Organisations and the Politics of Transformation* (London: Routledge, 1998), pp. 83–8.

> Increasingly, the effect of state funds on our community has been to neutralise its militancy . . . A whole generation of 'ethnic' workers and race relations experts has been born who are accountable not to the Black community but to the State which pays them. Their brief, however unwitting, is to keep the lid on the cauldron, and their existence is seen as proof of the governments 'concern' to soften the effects of its own institutionalised racism.[28]

More important than mapping the fortunes of every individual organisation, then, is analysing Antiracism from Above as an historically contingent strategy. In an era of unrest, its institutions can be compelled into playing an active role in political life; to appear as radical as the times demand. Absent that mass struggle, it settles into inertia. In turn, whereas the state may in times of social strife opt for the path of containment, it can quickly turn to coercion once it feels the balance of forces lie in its favour. We have seen this in real time from the way that Black Lives Matter bandwagon jumping has made way for firm state repression through augmentations in policing, both in the US and the UK.

Most of all then, through this process of NGOisation the *politics* of Black* politics was gradually drained out: the organisations of this new era could still form powerful insights of the problems engulfing their communities, but were left adrift without an overarching political theory to generate solutions. In its place came a corporate, depoliticised ethos; by the late 1990s the Campaign Against Racism and Fascism noted how this had become baked into Black* civil society:

---

28 Beverly Bryan, Stella Dadzie & Suzanne Scafe, *Heart of the Race: Black Women's Lives in Britain* (London & New York: Verso, 2018), p. 179.

> If you look through the documents, reports and newsletters coming from the Black Voluntary Sector, you do not read about raw racism which affects the most vulnerable among the black communities or even about campaigning. You read the same language of the marketplace which impregnates the White Voluntary Sector. It is about 'good practice', 'partnerships', 'service provision', going for 'consultations' and, above all, 'lobbying for resources.[29]

It is difficult to develop a grand theory of history when the future extends only as far as the next funding grant. And even harder to maintain a radical political orientation with council workers peering through your paperwork.

29 'What's happening in the voluntary sector?' *Campaign Against Racism and Fascism*, 37, (April/May 1997), pp. 10–11, accessed at https://irr.org.uk/app/uploads/2017/05/no.37.pdf (last accessed August 2021).

Chapter 5

New modes of organising: Culture, community and crisis

In this book, we have chosen to use the term 'antiracism' as a shorthand descriptor for work undertaken during the movements of the Black Power era. But it should be clear by now that the horizons of these movements extended far beyond a simple opposition to racism – these were struggles for community and self-determination, spanning campaigns for housing, labour, education, the family, anti-fascism and anti-state violence. They oriented themselves towards a more expansive ideal of liberation, building ecosystems of institutions, drawing upon radical ideological currents and locating themselves within a global struggle for decolonisation and against imperialism, in an attempt to construct a society that was fundamentally different – rather than simply a Britain which had varnished out the most violent excesses of racism.

In order to domesticate this radical project, this ecosystem of Black* political activism had to be broken up and dispersed in a way that they could be carefully managed as and when needed. Civil Society, Enterprise and the Politics of recognition were central to the process of smoothing out the antagonisms between racialised communities and the British state. These were the carrots dangled before racialised communities – all the while flanked by columns of police officers with sticks (and riot shields) held at the ready. In themselves, they also reflected the general orientation of a nascent neoliberalism that was taking shape under the new Conservative administrations.

Rather than an organic network of movements and institutions, what we had after 1981 increasingly resembled an assembly line of race relations initiatives – where antiracist work could continue in nominal form, albeit bound up in a web of dependencies and patronage with the institutions it sought to challenge. It was antiracism as a single-issue struggle; the antiracism of pundits and unconscious bias practitioners, of 'community leaders' and clientelism.

The racialised masses of Britain did not march mindlessly into moderation after 1981. Collective memories of poverty, exclusion and state brutality cannot simply be washed away with warm overtures from the government. But a movement is not merely an aimless mass of people; it is determined by institutions, organisers and ideology. The new strategic orientation of the times re-routed these away from their earlier radicalism, in the process changing the texture of antiracist organising at large. For those who stood the most to gain from this change – the careerists in the midst – the transition towards moderation and reform was rapid. Meanwhile others trying to navigate this new terrain with good intentions became gradually imprisoned by its contradictions – for them this change was less a leap of faith into the arms of local authorities, than finding themselves swallowed up by sinking sands.

To highlight the manifold predicaments post-1981 is not to idealise the violent antagonism that had characterised the relationship between racialised communities and the state prior to it, much less to fetishise the riot as the only meaningful form of political action.

It is merely to point out that Antiracism from Above ultimately did not – indeed, could not – deal with the root causes of this antagonism, but rather offered partial concessions to a segment of racialised communities that could quickly be rolled back once the times allowed.

Communities of resistance

Whether through the growth of enterprise, the politics of recognition or civil society, what the consolidation of Antiracism from Above most symbolised was the reorganisation of a radical Black* community that had come into formation over the decades prior.

Having been alienated from white Britain, radical sections of Black and Asian communities had pieced together a self-contained political and social lifeworld of their own. Built in the shadow of state neglect and social exclusion, this uneven and contradictory project eventually stirred into life as a constellation of political formations, self-help organisations and spaces, which provided the arterial networks through which legal defence campaigns, supplementary schooling, and strikes – like the one at Imperial Typewriters – could be sustained.

These networks were in turn nourished by a process of political education, leadership and the careful nurturing of a consciousness which reflected the radical upheaval of the times.

These forms and spaces had encountered naked hostility from the British state. High profile examples like that of The Mangrove Caribbean restaurant in West London – subject to a sustained campaign of police harassment, leading to the watershed Mangrove Nine court case, and eventually its closure

– stand alongside a litany of independent and community organisations persecuted out of existence. What Antiracism from Above and the developments of the 80s achieved was to pry open this radical ecosystem and re-route it into more manageable sections of the British political and cultural apparatus; councils, community 'projects' and cultural fetes.

No longer governed by the internal rhythm of racialised communities, Britain's radical milieu gradually became disciplined by the demands of capitalist society in its new institutional home. Denied both a pathway to major social transformation by the New Right, as well as the means through which to reproduce itself as a radical mode of organising, antiracist politics became institutionalised, ossified and eventually withered. In place of the difficult work of untangling the contradictions in their communities, activists were drawn into conflicts between their agendas and institutional demands. This is before even considering the more concrete ways in which racialised communities were broken up and dispersed through slum clearance and displacement – something that has continued apace since at least the 1960s. The 1978 documentary Blacks Britannica explores how such policies were advanced from the late 60s across English cities under the guise of preventing ghettoisation – and to avoid the emergence of Black rebellions as had been witnessed in the slums of the US. Meanwhile Runnymede Trust and CLASS's 2021 report, 'Pushed to the Margins', documented the rapid gentrification of boroughs across London during the 2010s, outlining the once-unthinkable transformation in the social character of sites like Peckham and Shoreditch.[1]

1 Adam Almeida, 'Pushed to the Margins: A Quantitative Analysis of Gentrification in London in the 2010s', Runnymede Trust & CLASS, available at https://runnymedetrust.org/projects-and-publications/employment-3/pushed-to-the-margins.html (last accessed August 2021).

The issue of consciousness, culture and the creation of radical communities were explored in earlier, less-remarked-upon works by Sivanandan, such as *Alien Gods* and *Black Power: The Politics of Existence*. Taken in this light, his strident rejection of developments during the 1980s, such as Labour Party Black Sections and the Black Trade Unionists Solidarity Movement, can be read less as a lament for a revolution that was most likely not waiting around the corner, than a requiem for a radical community coming undone. As just one example, Darcus Howe's political biography recounts the case of *Race Today* colleague Farrukh Dhondy being recruited as commissioning editor at Channel 4, during its early era of radical experimental TV. This saw Dhondy trying to use the opportunity – unthinkable a few years prior – as an extension of the political and communicative work of the *Race Today* journal, as well as securing a more public platform for Howe to sermonise to the masses. On the flipside, as Howe's media presence grew, his interest in *Race Today* waned. The journal came to an end in 1988, with the Collective following soon after[2] – depriving the political landscape of the 1990s of a vital voice.

We don't seek to romanticise the idea of racialised people permanently eking out a meagre existence on the edge of British society simply for the sake of preserving 'autonomy'. But the process of antiracism being 'plugged in' to mainstream political institutions irreversibly tied its fate up with theirs. Examples like Howe, Dhondy and *Race Today* are legion, and must be treated with the care and attention they deserve when we grapple with the difficult questions we encounter today: How can we exploit what appear to be small openings of oxygen in an otherwise suffocating political climate? How do we navigate the possibilities

2 See Robin Bunce & Paul Field's *Renegade: The Life and Times of Darcus Howe* (London: Bloomsbury, 2017), Chapter 17.

and contradictions thrown up by social and political realignment? To play blind to the risks is dangerous. To deny the allure is disingenuous.

Culture and its contradictions

Culture and cultural production – through literature, performances, arts and the study of history – is a vital component of radical campaigns, both as a form of communication and as a means of reproducing different ways of thinking and being. This is even more the case for movements of displaced and uprooted people, as will be found in antiracist organising.

Culture in the form of literature was central to the formation of the radical consciousness that underpinned the work of Black Power groups and crystallised into the political sensibility of 'Political Blackness'. Outfits like *Race Today* in turn worked to generate cultural production of their own to feed back to movements, dedicating sections of the journal to culture, and co-initiating the International Book Fair of Radical Black and Third World Books with New Beacon Books and Bogle-L'Ouverture Publications from 1982, which attracted an international audience. But culture is never without its contradictions, and there have always been tensions over the place of culture, the content of culture, and the aim of cultural production within movements.

What we understand as 'culture' can be broken down into different facets: the practice of culture, the ideology produced through culture, and the power these draw upon. Different configurations of these produce different outcomes. The practice of culture without consideration of ideology or power can become a hollow symbolism. This can be seen in the types of empty imagery churned out by the 'diversity' industry, or in the fact that all manner of people can swoon over the iconography of the Black Panthers while skipping over the matter of their Marxism-Leninism or Revolutionary Nationalism entirely. Practice and ideology without an analysis of power can, sometimes unwittingly, become reappropriated in the service of deeply reactionary politics.

This can even happen with some narrow cultural politics that seek ostensibly to counter white hegemony. There's no doubt that for formerly colonised or displaced people, seeking to recover, pre-colonial forms of culture and history can be an empowering exercise. Yet simply succumbing to the romance of pre-colonial history can end up valorising the prejudices and chauvinism that can permeate those pre-colonial histories too. Trying to simply leap back into history in the name of cultural authenticity in this way has become a way of legitimising unjust social hierarchies within communities and movements. This takes the form of subordinating women activists to particular social roles in the name of traditional gender norms, of justifying caste hierarchies, or other ethnic discriminations and so on. Culture can therefore hold a mirror to power, mystify power or mobilise power; and culture should therefore always be a plane of struggle, rather than taken as an unalloyed good.

While the capillaries of culture helped facilitate the growth of an expansive 'Politically Black' consciousness, narrow culturalist ideas of race and ethnicity facilitated its decline. This is best evidenced by the work of academic Tariq Modood, whose broadsides against 'Political Blackness' as 'harming Asians' in Britain during the late 80s/early 90s continue to be referenced as the definitive word on the framework to this day.[3] This is deeply

3 Namely Tariq Modood, '"Black", racial equality and Asian identity', *Journal of Ethnic and Migration Studies*, 14:3, pp. 397–404, (1998); and Tariq Modood, 'Political Blackness and British Asians', *Sociology*, 28:4, (1994), pp. 859–76.

unfortunate, given how Modood's critiques rest on a conservative reconceptualisation of antiracism as rooted in the task of developing cultural pride for Asians 'by virtue of the hard work and disciplined commitment that we or our parents have made [in Britain]'.[4]

Accordingly, he cleaves apart the issues of 'racial discrimination', 'cultural discrimination' and class discrimination in such a way as to pit concerns of African-Caribbean communities against Asian communities in some quite distasteful ways – including by dismissing 'attempts to [get policy makers] to focus on the equality of treatment of offenders by the criminal justice system' as broadly irrelevant to Asians. His criticisms centred the post-1981 form of institutionalised antiracism that we have ourselves challenged here, but his are steeped in wounded defensiveness at the supposed sins of African-Caribbean antiracists. It clearly sought to jettison the radical antiracist history that preceded this period, rather than try to recover or build upon it – and conceals a barely veiled satisfaction that the decline of 'Political Blackness' may 'in retrospect be seen as marking the limit of the influence of militant anti-racism' in favour of a liberal multiculturalism.

What the shift post-1981, and particularly with the advent of state multiculturalism, did was to decouple culture from the process of community and movement-building and turn it into a product, or merely a depoliticised object of entertainment. To use the popular phrase – 'culture' became repackaged as 'saris, steel pans and samosas', often on the payroll of local authorities. The allocation of funding is never a neutral process, and often serves to prop up certain types of organisations and ideologies

4 It is also something of a confused argument – while railing against the 'essentialism' of 'Political Blackness', he defines Asians in the 1988 article curiously as 'Roughly, [those] people who believe that the Taj Mahal is an object of their history.'

over others – namely those that are more conservative, conciliatory or culturally inclined. As one pamphlet on Black Power in Brixton noted: 'Cultural nationalism' perhaps had a stronger appeal at the time, but its susceptability [sic] to being co-opted, funded, and institutionalised by the leftwing element of the local state was maybe much greater than the more uncompromising class positions of the [Black Unity and Freedom Party].'[5]

To take an example, the first Black History Month (BHM) celebration, organised in London in October 1987 was developed and supported through the Greater London Council and, following the GLC's dissolution, the London Strategic Policy Unit. Led by former GLC project coordinator Akyaaba Addai-Sebo, the affair was marked by a distinctly Afrocentric and cultural bent[6] rather than the socialist currents that had permeated other contemporary antiracist organisations. Furthermore, the Month's inaugural address was delivered by the notorious Ron Karenga, originator of the Kwanzaa celebration and co-founder of the US Organization[7] – the California-based Black cultural-nationalist organisation that found themselves in bitter, and sometimes bloody, conflict with the local Black Panther Party. More scandalous still was Karenga's history as a police asset as part of the FBI'S COINTELPRO programme, and his imprisonment for torturing women in US Organization. It was certainly something of an inauspicious opening to Britain's Black History Month tradition.

5 https://pasttenseblog.wordpress.com/2021/04/09/in-the-shadow-of-the-spg-racist-policing-resistance-black-power-in-1970s-brixton (last accessed August 2021).

6 https://crer.scot/post/2017/09/28/how-did-black-history-month-come-to-the-uk (last accessed August 2021).

7 https://blackagendareport.com/why-i-dont-do-kwaanza (last accessed August 2021).

In the years since, efforts to institute Black History Month as a feature in the British cultural calendar have, perhaps inevitably, encountered the range of issues inherent in mainstreaming such initiatives. Come October every year, anecdotes are plentiful of well-meaning teachers using BHM to rehash the well-worn redemption arc of the (US) civil rights struggle, or of public institutions hosting polite-if-pedestrian cultural celebrations. But as the 'race question' has grown more salient in Britain, BHM has increasingly been used as a prime opportunity for corporations, climate polluters and cops to profess their supposed commitment to diversity, inclusion and representation – while also serving as an annual cash injection for individual opportunists.

The revenge of representation politics

On 7 May 2021, Sadiq Khan was declared the winner of the London mayoral election, allowing him to maintain his 'historic' position as the city's first Muslim mayor.

Ten years prior, the city had erupted in the largest uprising of its kind since 1981, after the police killing of Mark Duggan in North London. In the decade since, the morbid arithmetic of deaths in police custody has increased by 376, one-fifth of them at the hands of London's Metropolitan police.[8] Then-mayor Boris Johnson, who responded to the uprisings with a suite of policing powers to criminalise Black youth, now serves as Conservative Prime Minister of the country. Then-Director of Public Prosecutions Keir Starmer, who ran all-night courts to facilitate draconian prosecutions of those youths, now serves as Leader of the Labour Party that Khan represents.

---

8 https://inquest.org.uk/deaths-in-police-custody (last accessed November 2021).

Sixteen years prior to the election, Brazilian Jean Charles de Menezes was shot dead at Stockwell tube station in a counter-terror operation – with officers having mis-identified him as a Muslim terror suspect on account of his 'Mongolian eyes'.[9] Denied justice or accountability, de Menezes' loved ones would be forced to look on as the commander in charge of the operation, Cressida Dick, rose through the ranks to become the first woman Commissioner of the Metropolitan Police, lauded by Khan as an 'historic day for London'.[10]

In this way, the injustices and brutalities of racism that disfigure the social landscape of Britain are airbrushed from sight. In their place, supposed 'wins', such as the election of decidedly milquetoast mayoral candidates of colour – or for that matter, Black politicians to the White House – are repurposed to serve as shoddy proxies of social progress. As representation politics have become more widely embraced by the mainstream in places like Britain and America, they have increasingly become unmoored from their history in antiracist struggle, and cut off from any forms of self-organisation. The shift in priority towards representation politics and mainstream party politicking has had a profound impact on the way people understand or relate to the ideas of collective antiracist organising, and how they mobilise towards that end – sometimes with disastrous consequences.

In 1981, the district of Handsworth in North West Birmingham exploded as part of the wave of uprisings that summer. When Handsworth was again aflame in the 1985 uprisings, reports from that episode suggested hints of an inter-ethnic undertone this time round, with some attacks by African-Carib-

9 https://theguardian.com/commentisfree/2015/nov/18/shoot-to-kill-terror-fear-prejudice-jean-charles-de-menezes (last accessed August 2021).

10 https://theguardian.com/uk-news/2017/feb/22/cressida-dick-appointed-first-female-met-police-commissioner (last accessed August 2021).

bean youth apparently directed at Asian shopkeepers.[11] Twenty years on, the adjoining district of Lozells saw the crushing nadir of race riots between Blacks and Asians, sparked by the rumour of the rape of a young Black girl by Asian men.

Lozells 2005 was, and remains, the bleakest illustration of a growing divide between racialised groups in Britain. A renewed antiracist movement in Britain today cannot elide this issue. But to rebuild one requires a more meaningful discussion about the material roots of this division and the disparities between different ethnic groups in the country.

The fate of Lozells is bound up with the fate of its antiracist movements. Through the 1960s and 70s, the city of Birmingham was home to groups like the Midlands Indian Workers Association-GB (IWA-GB), which under the leadership of Jagmohan Joshi was among the most avowedly Marxist of the various IWAs. Rejecting the lure of state funding, wedded to a socialist analysis of antiracism rooted in workers' struggles, and committed to Black-Asian solidarity – as demonstrated by Jagmohan's role in establishing the Black People's Alliance – it was a model of the organising of the Black Power era. His premature death in 1979 – mere weeks after Thatcher's rise to power – marked the end of an era and a grim allegory of the times. After his passing, the IWA-GB's membership declined, while its prestige and influence among other Black and Asian groups faded. By

11 See for example Ellis Cashmore, 'The Handsworth Riots', *Marxism Today*, 29:10, (1985), accessed at banmarchive.org.uk/collections/mt/index_frame.htm (last accessed August 2021); The Handsworth Riots Oct 85 & 'HOME AFFAIRS. Civil disorder: Scarman Report on the 1981 Brixton riots; part 2', PREM 19/1521, Records of the Prime Minister's Office: Correspondence and Papers, 1979–1997, held at: Kew: The National Archives. Alternative assessments emphasising growing class antagonisms can be found in, for example, Ambalavener Sivanandan, 'UK commentary', *Race & Class*, 27:3, (1986), pp. 81–5; and Anandi Ramamurthy, *Black Star: Britain's Asian Youth Movements* (London: Pluto, 2013), p. 160.

1980/81 the organisation had made its first council grant bid,[12] while members grew more comfortable with the Labour Party, in some instances becoming elected representatives.[13]

When one of the present authors lived in Birmingham, the disparity between Asian – particularly Pakistani, sometimes Bangladeshi – elected representatives and Black representatives was a source of tension that simmered in the open. Connected to this was dissatisfaction at the perceived stability that this level of representation afforded the Asians in terms of a community infrastructure. And topping this off was the spectre of the racist Asian shopkeeper fleecing Black communities.

And yet, ultimately, none of these social facts have done much to remedy the grinding deprivation which blights the lives of Birmingham's largely working-class Pakistani and Bangladeshi populations. Nor has it ameliorated the fact that they face the highest unemployment rates in the city, or the lowest rates of professional qualifications.[14] The warm glow of seeing their skinfolk reflected in the city council offers little comfort for the one-third of them living in homes without central heating. And political representation certainly hasn't saved them from their status as contemporary folk devils in the British public imagination – where Pakistanis in Birmingham have become synonymous with menacing Muslim 'extremists'.

Community infrastructure is certainly a vital element of self-reliance. But the infrastructure that exists for Pakistanis and Bangladeshis in Birmingham is itself thoroughly compromised; the networks of mosques at its heart have largely been recruited to the service of a counterterror apparatus that criminalises

12 Albeit later withdrawn.

13 Ramamurthy, *Black* Star, p. 160.

14 Alessio Cangiano, 'Mapping of Race and Poverty in Birmingham' (Barrow Cadbury Trust, 2007).

those communities. And the canalisation of Asian political energy into local party politics over the last few decades has led to the decay of independent political self-organisation. In short, the privilege of representation primarily benefited those elected individuals and a circle living under the shade of crony politics in the city: 'community leaders', their fellow outriders – and those dodgy shopkeepers.

By pointing this out we don't intend to patronise Black communities of Birmingham with the lesson that *all that glitters is not gold* – and certainly not to undermine the dire reality of their social distress, or wave away racism they experience at the hands of their ethnic counterparts. The point is to stress that Birmingham is no localised phenomenon: the last 40 years has shown that the promotion of political 'representation' almost only ever privileges rank opportunism, no more. It is to underscore the fact that there exists in Birmingham, as across Britain, an objective basis for inter-ethnic solidarity rooted in the similarities of conditions: the unity of empty bellies and of overcrowded homes; the torment of an unbearable present and uncertain futures. What clearly needs work is the subjective basis for solidarity; the desire for it. That requires an organising process to nurture it.

Absent a common political agenda, independent self-organisation or democratic institutions in which to deepen struggle, solidarity itself has become brittle and at times, bitter. Representation politics often rein in broader political visions, and the politics of resource scarcity and inter-ethnic rivalries reign over radical antiracist organising. One wonders if even the Labour Party Black Sections could be replicated today, or whether they would implode on impact given the level of division and stratification among racialised communities in Britain.

Fated for defeat?

There is little use indulging in counterfactuals: we cannot in retrospect predict whether a militant, grassroots Antiracism from Below would have been able to weather Thatcherism's assault on radical politics any more than the labour movement could. Nor can we tell whether the insurrectionary promise imputed into struggles of that era by contemporaries would have come to fruition, had they not gone down the path of institutionalisation and professionalisation after 1981.

Perhaps, even, the fluidity and radical community-based organising of the Black Power groups were both a strength and fatal weakness: their inability to scale up into durable national organisations may have left the door open for the professionalised antiracism of the 1980s to step into the breach. On the other hand, examples such as the dissolution of national groups like OWAAD and the failed attempts to form a National Asian Youth Movement underscore the difficulties of developing and maintaining radical institutions at scale.

However, one thing is clear: our understanding of the struggles and defeats in the post-1981 period must go beyond a simple story of 'selling out' by activists. Such a narrow analysis both understates the deep difficulties that period threw up – not least the ongoing repression of radical organising – and implicitly it overstates our ability to transcend similar obstacles today. The dilemmas we have to grapple with today are just as tough as those that organisers confronted decades ago: what different forms does struggle take in an era of retreat, and how far can we go without consigning ourselves to defeat? To state the obvious, struggle is hard. Any assessment of the post-1981 era should be approached as a strategic question rather than a purely moralistic one.

Similarly, we would do best to avoid presenting the issues that emerged within antiracism in this period as though the problem lies solely at the feet of a cabal of middle-class Blacks and Asians leading the masses astray. As outlined above, we acknowledge and in large part support the critiques of the emerging Black and brown petit bourgeoisie who found organised expression in the 1980s. Yet, we are wary of missing the wood for the trees; of over-emphasising middle-class mischief at the expense of analysing how and why they were able to emerge as a political bloc. It would also be remiss of us to ignore the bad-faith accusations of middle-class status being levelled at women of colour by their male counterparts at the time – less by way of analysis, and more as ad hominem to undermine them, or deflect from issues around patriarchal culture. As Amrit Wilson has explained it, 'any woman that became articulate was suddenly labelled middle class, no matter what her or her parents' background' – including by individuals who could reasonably be defined as 'middle class' themselves.[15] The Brixton Black Women's Group also rebuffed more mechanical forms of this argument, questioning, 'Since when did access to education and the fact that we may occupy "middle class" jobs automatically lead to petty bourgeois politics?'[16]

And finally, the retreat of the left and radicals during this period ought not be individualised as down to their 'betrayal' of their historical responsibilities. Their defeat formed part of an international reorientation towards the forces of the right and a second wind for global capitalism that set much of the organised left back by decades.

Ultimately, while Thatcherism offered a worldmaking project of class power, radical forces were grappling with crisis politics:

15 Ramamurthy, *Black Star*, p. 110.

16 Sudbury, *Other Kinds of Dreams*, pp. 159.

defensive struggles in the face of a right-wing renaissance. As Thatcher's carnival of reaction marched grimly onwards through the 80s, forces on the left retreated from vibrant struggle towards the task of stitching together a patchwork rainbow coalition for the Labour Party come next election. To critique the direction taken by antiracists after 1981 is not to suggest that, with one more heave, radical street movements could have overturned the British state under Thatcher. Nor is it born out of a starry-eyed nostalgia for the good old days of Black Power. It is merely to emphasise the lessons that can be taken, the errors that should be forsaken, and how to apply them now – when a new, hauntingly familiar political crisis has awakened.

Chapter 6

Between rebellion and reaction

Today it's clear that we are, in more ways than one, living in the afterlives of 1981. Those in power evince a grim nostalgia for the days of Thatcherism, while summoning up its worst spectres from their shallow graves: far-right flirtations and unabashed racism, ratcheting up law and order and tightening down national borders. Seizing the reins of a Britain in deep crisis and political polarisation, the Johnson government, like Thatcher's, emerged as an expression of a right-wing renaissance, eager and willing to flex its muscles of coercion and crush an emergent British left.

Meanwhile, just shy of 40 years since the 1981 rebellions, the youth of Britain exploded in summer 2020 as part of the worldwide Black Lives Matters-inspired protests. The demonstrations were historic in proportion and impressively well-honed in their politics – homemade placards held aloft at the demos indicted the British state for its own racist crimes, and memorialised individuals killed at its hands.

Across 260 cities, towns and villages, protests sparked by the police murder of George Floyd saw placards proclaiming that 'The UK is not innocent'. The names of those killed by British police were scattered across signs: names like Joy Gardner, killed in 1993 in an immigration raid which saw 13 feet of tape wrapped around her head. Or Sean Rigg, brutalised and left to die at the entrance of Brixton Police station after a mental health episode in 2008. Christopher Alder, the former paratrooper who choked on his own blood in 1998 in a police station after a head injury, as the officers made monkey noises around him. And Sarah Reed, found dead in her cell in Holloway prison in 2016, two years after being assaulted by a police officer. The list goes on – running to over 1,800 people killed after contact with the police since 1990.[1]

Faced with these mass demonstrations, the Johnson government initiated an investigation by the *Commission on Race and Ethnic Disparities* headed by Tony Sewell, also known as the Sewell report. Whereas Scarman had dismissed the existence of 'institutional racism' outright four decades earlier, the Sewell report danced around definitions, and fretted over the apparent overuse of the term. And chief among its recommendations was the evergreen call to 'Create police workforces that represent the communities they serve'.[2]

But society's pendulum does not swing smoothly back and forth. In periods of crisis it jerks erratically between rebellion and reaction. And it carries with it the congealed weight of history. The social rupture this time round is not a clean mirror image of the 1980s, and is indelibly marked by the developments post-1981.

The fate of antiracism from above

One such development was the fact that representation politics had, by 2020, reached their obscene zenith: the government Cabinet that the demonstrations were directed against was among the most diverse in history, and among its most rabidly

1 https://inquest.org.uk/deaths-in-police-custody (last accessed November 2021).

2 https://sgov.uk/government/publications/the-report-of-the-commission-on-race-and-ethnic-disparities/summary-of-recommendations (last accessed September 2021).

racist. The Home Secretary in charge of policing was the daughter of East African Indian migrants, while the head of the Sewell commission was himself a descendant of the famed Windrush generation. This itself reflects the fragmentation of a radical Black* political sensibility in the decades since 1981 and the rise of a more assertively conservative Black and brown middle class. But most striking is witnessing how, in the post-1981 moment, the fate of British antiracism became so entwined with the fate of British liberalism – such that the present crisis of liberalism also means a crisis in multicultural antiracism.

Following the 2007–8 economic crash, the tide across Europe turned against state multiculturalism. Already worn thin by political and media fearmongering of 'Muslim extremists' and 'illegal immigrants' in the early years of the new millennium, Britain's multicultural facade of 'tolerance' and 'diversity' collapsed in on itself in the aftermath of the crash. In its place emerged a new ideological consensus that lurches ever rightward.

Speaking on the same day as the then-largest mobilisation of the English Defence League, Conservative Prime Minister David Cameron joined fellow European leaders by announcing that state multiculturalism had 'failed' in February 2011. State multiculturalism had, in his words, created a climate for 'extremism' by '[encouraging] different cultures to live separate lives, apart from each other and apart from the mainstream . . . [and tolerating] these segregated communities behaving in ways that run completely counter to our values.'[3]

Within a few short years the economic crisis had hardened into a political crisis in Britain, symbolised by the break from the European Union and the fragmentation of domestic party-political alliances. The latest Conservative administration under Boris

3 https://gov.uk/government/speeches/pms-speech-at-munich-security-conference (last accessed September 2021).

Johnson has seized the moment to push for an institutional reorganisation of Britain, while shifting ever further away from the post-war liberal consensus. In order to consolidate a political base in support of this shift, the government has dispensed with the polite racism of multiculturalism in favour of frequent appeals to the most reactionary impulses of white nationalism in Britain – including through divisive 'Culture War' tactics aimed at folk devils like 'Critical Race Theory' or 'wokeness'.

What the Culture War trades on is the disconnect between the representation of antiracism – in the case of universities, those vestiges of liberal multiculturalism lingering in the academy, for example – and the institutional weakness of antiracist practice in Britain. In doing so the government, alongside a compliant media, can exaggerate the strength of antiracism in Britain, and in turn use that as a pretence to secure greater control and expand their ideological hegemony over universities, and other spaces.

What, then, is the state of our antiracism today – caught between a crumbling consensus and a new Britain taking form?

The BAME blame game

In the summer of 2020 we witnessed how the hope and promise of the Black Lives Matter protests offline soon devolved into a fractious debate about the term 'BAME' (Black, Asian and Minority Ethnic) online.[4]

---

4 In this context we wrote our article, 'Strained Solidarities: On (re)building a mass anti-racist movement in Britain', for *Ceasefire Magazine* to trace out some of the dynamics that we describe in this: https://ceasefiremagazine.co.uk/strained-solidarities-rebuilding-mass-anti-racist-movement-britain (last accessed September 2021). Miriyam Aouragh's *'White privilege' and shortcuts to anti-racism* explores the dynamics which have produced this, and the consequences for antiracist solidarity: https://journals.sagepub.com/doi/full/10.1177/0306396819874629 (last accessed September 2021).

The controversy over the use of 'BAME' to refer to non-white people in Britain creeps to the top of British Twitter trending topics and mainstream media op-ed pages, it seems, every other season. More often than not it centres on 'disparities' between the experiences of different groups captured under the acronym – particularly on the differential levels of representation afforded to these groups – and on the issue of racism between groups under the BAME umbrella. In the context of the 2020 debate, it also focused on the question of whether the racism affecting Black people should be decoupled from racism affecting all other non-white groups in Britain.[5]

It is little use having this discussion in the abstract, or at the level of terminology alone, without considering the organisational and political undercurrents that inform it. In part, the 'BAME' debate points back to the complex tensions between self-organisation and 'separatism' that we discuss further in Chapter 12. But more fundamentally it relates to shifting ideas about the nature, form and value of collective political organisation in a time when lobby-style multicultural politics have declined, without being properly replaced by a concrete practical alternative.

If 'Political Blackness' was – initially – the ideological expression of Black Power, then BAME can be understood as the ideological expression of multiculturalism. In essence, 'BAME' represents a form of top-down 'collectivism' that lends itself to

---

5 https://theguardian.com/commentisfree/2019/aug/09/black-people-racism-anti-blackness-discrimination-minorities (last accessed May 2021). Much of this discourse appears to have been informed or influenced by the theory and/or language associated with 'Afropessimism', descended from the North American academy and circulated in large part through social media. Annie Olaloku-Teriba's essay, 'Afro-Pessimism and the (Un)Logic of Anti-Blackness' is required reading on the problems with this framework: https://historicalmaterialism.org/articles/afro-pessimism-and-unlogic-anti-blackness (last accessed September 2021).

the mechanisms of an antiracism from above. There are therefore many compelling reasons to oppose 'BAME' – we ourselves critique it as a term of the state and market, inorganic to the world of radical antiracist organising and more at home in the bureaucracy of ethnic lobby politics.

But the dominant arguments against BAME – or at least, those that find their way into the columns of the *Metro*, *Independent* and *Huffington Post* – approach it from a very different perspective. To give a flavour of the debate, one of the many think pieces published during summer 2020 lamented that the use of BAME masked the lack of Black Tories in the government. Others posited that racism directed by other non-white groups against Black people made 'BAME solidarity' impossible. The prevailing line of argument seemed to rail against the idea of a collective antiracist organisation – something that has waned over decades as the sphere of individualism has expanded, while the politics of social transformation made way for a form of patronage-fuelled lobby politics.

Collective struggle requires not just an aggregation of individuals but a political consciousness to bind them to a joint project – similar to the distinction made by Marx between the working class as a *class in itself* and as a *class for itself*; i.e. consciously organising as a class. That cannot be synthetically produced by any linguistic choice, but is an organic outgrowth of struggle. For a generation or more who have had very limited opportunities for mass political activity, collective self-organisation can instead decay into an exercise in rational self-interest. Therefore it may seem intuitively appealing to close ranks around immediate ethnic or social groups, to agitate around their immediate concerns, and to look out for self, rather than engage in the more complex work of building outwards to realise a more expansive antiracist project. We can also see this from the way that many anti-BAME arguments have blurred effortlessly into opposition towards any umbrella term for non-white people – be it BAME, 'people of colour' or otherwise – and into critiques of the very concept of multiracial organising. Rather than broadening out into a critique of Antiracism from Above, or the deep failures of state multiculturalism and the need for more radical forms of campaigning, much of the debate around BAME today ends up locked within the very same logic.

It reinforces the notion that the only remedies for racial injustice are found through appeals to the government and market, that there are a finite amount of resources available to do so, and that different communities must compete in a zero-sum game for these resources.

Based on this premise, drawing connections between similar-if-different forms of racism affecting different ethnic groups becomes a threat – it dilutes claims to specific injustice, rather than giving them texture. Accordingly, to organise across racial boundaries against racism in a more expansive sense would be to deny the specificities of experiences, rather than to deepen an analysis of racism.[6] It is also perhaps telling that, while the Sewell report was roundly condemned, the least contentious aspect would probably be its recommendation to 'Stop using aggregated and unhelpful terms such as 'BAME', to better focus on understanding disparities and outcomes for specific ethnic groups'.[7] And seemingly without any consideration as to precisely

6 It goes without saying that there are times when specificity should be foregrounded – for example, when challenging disparate experiences for specific groups of people within the healthcare sector. But equally, the overarching imperative of antiracist organising should bend towards broad-based collective struggle which foregrounds solidarity and fights for social transformation.

7 https://gov.uk/government/publications/the-report-of-the-commission-on-race-and-ethnic-disparities/summary-of-recommendations (last accessed September 2021).

why a project of such a fanatically right-wing government would be invested in breaking up even the modest, problematic form of collectivism embedded in 'BAME'. The response of Runnymede Trust head Halima Begum to the report applies as much to Tony Sewell as some of the more over-enthusiastic critics of BAME: 'If advice on the use of the term BAME is . . . the most pressing of its recommendations, then Britain's ethnic minority communities are being insulted by this report and its authors'.[8]

The emphasis placed on 'disparities and outcomes' in Sewell's recommendation is also illuminating. The dominance of disparity discourse as the yardstick of racism is central to the BAME debate, but itself often leads to a strategic dead end: is the issue that Black and brown people are 'disproportionately' victims of murderous police violence, or the very fact that these institutions have amassed the power to inflict such brutality over our lives? It is a framing of racism that focuses on the form of racist violence rather than its social function, and merely seeks to equalise ethnic disparities to a baseline level through technical fixes rather than political solutions.

Perhaps the issue lies less with the limitations of our collective language, and more with our jaundiced grammar of justice. Our aspirations urgently need to extend beyond equal-opportunity oppression.

In one way, the BAME blame game can be read as a distraction – an unnecessarily polarising red herring fanned by the media to divert attention from more glaring issues of racism. But in other ways, it appears more as a distillation of many dangerous tendencies and fault lines etched into antiracist discourse today. It cuts to the heart of what antiracism means and looks like, which must be addressed in our present moment.

8 https://theguardian.com/politics/2021/mar/29/boris-johnsons-race-commission-to-scrap-use-of-bame-label (last accessed September 2021).

Liberalism in revolt

If British antiracism became entwined with the fate of British liberalism what, then, became of the layer of professional antiracists whose fates were tethered to multiculturalism and Antiracism from Above? Their position was predicated on a grand compromise with the state: as long as they did not rock the boat they could be elevated as authentic interlocutors of their communities, and as long as the state afforded some sops to those communities these professionals had no reason to rock the boat. Therefore they were able to operate as custodians of a 'trickle-down antiracism', such that their personal advances could be projected as wins for the community, while challenges to their privileged positions – say, the denial of career progression, or loss of government support – were fashioned as *threats* that demanded the community's utmost attention. The political crises over the last decade has presented this layer of professionals with both predicaments and possibilities. To start with, the steady bifurcation of mainstream politics since the 2007/08 crisis has seen them increasingly frozen in an era that no longer exists, disconnected from the needs of their communities and out of step with the new political realities.

On one hand, they are being outflanked by the emergence of a political tendency avowedly to their right, with the rise of conservatives of colour that define themselves explicitly against multiculturalism.[9] As national politics have become more rigidly polarised in recent years, this conservative tendency has grown more hard-line in step with it, and can often be found lurking in the annals of *Spiked!*, unheard and increasingly the mainstream media too. On the other hand they are being challenged

9 Paul Warmington, 'The emergence of black British social conservatism', *Ethnic and Racial Studies*, 38:7, (2015), pp. 1152–68.

from below by a generation of Black and brown youth steeled by years of political desertion and declining social standards, pushed towards a post-multicultural radicalism – albeit without always being able to articulate this radicalism into a clear political programme.

In spite of the twin challenges they face, what the professional antiracists have in their favour is outsized access to a media apparatus still ready and willing to afford them a platform – allowing them to masquerade as the authentic voice of Black and brown struggle in Britain, and enabling them to shape the demands of antiracism today. Stirred into action as much by threats to their social position as by the increase in racism, today's professional antiracists have reinvented themselves as reborn rebels, raging against Brexit, Donald Trump or the excesses of Boris Johnson. Having found their latest muses, yet unable to stomach a transformative politics to match, they can instead be found taking to Twitter threads and *Guardian* op-eds, threading together a confused patchwork of ideologies – marrying liberal dictums with radical-sounding buzzwords cribbed from the left.

How else are we to explain the phenomenon whereby those propped up as antiracist thought leaders can wax lyrical about 'white supremacy' in the abstract, but wither on the vine when it comes to the question of political economy? Or issue stinging denunciations of racism at home, yet read from the same script as the government on matters of foreign policy?

The disconnect in priorities is stark. While working-class Black and brown communities struggle over the daily battles of poverty, the media is found fawning over campaigns to get a brown face on banknotes. Mass movements against the vast over-representation of Black people murdered by the state make way for campaigns against their under-representation in Oscar nominations. While people of colour abroad are suffocated by the weight of British imperial misadventure, antiracist 'thought leaders' in Britain agonise over their reasons for accepting *Order of the British Empire* honours.

Meanwhile, the rise of social media as the preeminent mode of organising today has intersected with the demise of antiracist organisations over the last decade of austerity in Britain. Out of this crucible has emerged a new actor on the antiracist scene: the influencer. This influencer 'class' heightens the existing tendencies of individualism, opportunism, competition and careerism circulating in the world of professionalised antiracism. Authority is conferred upon individuals who have no organic links with antiracist campaigning or organising credentials – but rather whose legitimacy is determined by social media follower counts. This is enabled by the way that social media reduces the issue of ideology to a checkbox exercise of threading together the right terms to appear 'good on x, y and z', which in turn feeds into the air of unearned authority that permeates online discourse. This moves the imperative even further from building a movement towards building a brand. We witnessed this come to a head during and since the 2020 Black Lives Matter demonstrations. Whether appearing on Uber ads while gig economy workers died on the job from exposure to Coronavirus, or drawing in tens of thousands of pounds on Gofundme pages to subsidise, among other things, police workshops – 'influencers' could be found tripping over themselves to show that, despite all their posturing for social change, it was the pocket change that mattered.

Seasoned activist Darcus Howe, by then known for his role in the Mangrove Nine trial and Race Today Collective, was elected by his peers to head the New Cross Massacre Action Committee's work, alongside founder of New Beacon Books John La Rose. Yet how would these respected veterans have fared against today's influencers at the vanguard – or rather, who would have commanded the respect of the masses today: those steeped in the graft, or deep in their grift?

Whether cultivating Black and brown entrepreneurs in the 1980s or elevating influencers today: the goal is less to change the reality of deprivation than the perception of it. What is needed now is a project of developing antiracism as a framework for liberation, placing it back within a wider analysis of power, capitalism and imperialism and imbuing it with the political substance that it is often emptied of – not least over the past four decades.

Chapter 7

The other internationalism

> The [Socialist International],[1] permeated through and through with bourgeois culture and led by a handful of political dilettantes, underestimated the whole importance of the colonial question. The world outside simply did not exist as far as they were concerned.[. . .]
>
> Instead of supporting the revolutionary movement in the colonies both materially and morally, [they] themselves became imperialists. – Manabendra Nath (MN) Roy, 1920[2]

> Is this strategy designed to allow the populations of the developed world to capture more of the growth projected over the next 5–15 years, if necessary at the cost of China, India and Brazil having to find new ways to break out of the middle income trap?[. . .] For me the answer is yes.[. . .]

1 The organisation of predominantly European socialist, social democratic and labour parties active between 1889–1916, also known as the 'Second International'. This was succeeded by the Communist International (Comintern) – aka the 'Third International' – which placed a much greater emphasis on the colonial question. For more on this see Vijay Prashad's essay, *The Internationalist Lenin: Self-determination and anti-colonialism:* https://mronline.org/2020/08/10/the-internationalist-lenin-self-determination-and-anti-colonialism/ (last accessed August 2021).

2 Manabendra Nath Roy, *Supplementary Theses on the National and Colonial Questions* in *Liberate the Colonies! Communism and Colonial Freedom 1917–1924* ed. John Riddell, Vijay Prashad & Nazeef Mollah (New Delhi: Leftword Books, [1918] 2019).

> It is a programme to deliver growth and prosperity in Wigan, Newport and Kirkcaldy – if necessary at the price of not delivering them to Shenzhen, Bombay and Dubai. – Paul Mason, 2018[3]

In Britain, the vitality of Black Power drew from its attempt to ignite the political consciousness of the most alienated sections of British society, and to articulate a response to the structure of power in Britain defined by race/class/citizenship. It was also significant for integrating a radical internationalist politics that much of the British left had long left out in the cold.

The efforts to incorporate racialised communities into the sphere of Britishness over the decades has been used to try and disarm this radical internationalist sensibility. Similar strategies had been tried and tested elsewhere, sometimes with devastating effect.

Wedged between World War Two and the invasion of Vietnam, the Korean War is often banished from the record, recast as the 'Forgotten War' of the US. But for the Korean people, their memories seared with the experience, the war was marked by two enduring facts of history. Firstly, the fact that the war was the US army's first foray as a racially desegregated force, following President Harry Truman's Executive Order 9981 in 1948. Secondly, that this multicultural military force turned North Korea into one of the most-bombed countries in the world, evaporating nearly one-fifth of the population and flattening virtually every town.

Truman's Executive Order 9981 was embraced as a watershed by a number of mainstream civil organisations and leaders, and Black participation in the war was welcomed as a stepping stone

3 https://neweconomics.opendemocracy.net/kind-capitalism-possible-left-build (last accessed August 2021).

towards greater domestic advances for Blacks in America. But other contemporaries refused the idea that the Black American rite of passage would be written in the blood of foreigners.

Outraged by the disconnect between his own experiences travelling in Asia at the time, and the uncritical embrace of US imperial endeavours by sections of the Black press, radical journalist William Worthy issued a withering response in the pages of the Washington Afro-American. In it, he condemned the Black political establishment for their failure to 'raise the roof about white supremacy and [the] imperialistic premises [of the war]' as an indictment of how 'narrowly defined and internationally myopic'[4] their politics were. Worthy's critique of what would shortly become the leadership of the Civil Rights movement highlights the central dividing line of antiracist struggles rooted in the Global North, which would in turn shape the divide between Civil Rights and the Black Power era in the US.

The question posed was simple: would those struggles focus narrowly on the inclusion of disenfranchised groups within the boundaries of the national body politic – or would they transcend those boundaries, and adopt a global view of racism and antiracism that puts anti-imperialism at its centre?

Indigenising antiracism

Central to the task of containing the radical project of Black Power after 1981 was incorporating Black* politics into the fold of Britishness to a degree it had hitherto been denied – and whose exclusion had made Black Power such a potent challenge to the status quo. In other words, it meant 'indigenising' Black* politics, and therefore domesticating it.

4 Robeson Taj Frazier, *The East is Black: Cold War China in the Black Radical Imagination* (Durham: Duke University Press, 2013), p. 80.

This saw the new generation of 'native' Black and brown citizens drawn into a fragile zone of inclusion within British social and political life – as opposed to their immigrant parents, perpetually cast out on the peripheries. This strategy of inclusion allowed for a fragmentation of antiracist struggles, by pitting communities against one another in the race to be embraced by society as 'good British citizens' with legitimate claims to make, while paving the way for racism to be reorganised and redeployed against others.

In addition to this, the manner in which movements defined their objectives from the latter end of the 1980s onwards reflected the shift towards a civic antiracism – which came to be gradually, if never exclusively, preoccupied with the fate of non-white people within Britain. It also indicated a mellowing of ambitions from the revolutionary fervour of the late 1960s–70s, with a very different form of internationalism prevailing in this period, as discussed below.

In the early 1970s, a pamphlet by the Black Liberation Front outlined their rather ambitious beliefs on the role of racialised people in Britain as such:

> [Minority] revolution or even a minority uprising [in Britain] in conjunction with revolutionary warfare in our home countries is a course that might well have to be considered as expedient for our survival . . . *In the cause of survival for Black people all over the world, the Third World minorities in Britain should even contemplate supreme revolutionary sacrifice* (emphasis added).[5]

5 'Revolutionary Black Nationalism: A paper for discussion', WONG/6/40, *Papers of Ansel Wong*, held at: London: Black Cultural Archives.

Referring to a provisional constitution of the abortive National Asian Youth Movement put together a decade later, Anandi Ramamurthy described the fact that

> while opposing colonialism and the struggle of oppressed nations, [it] made no mention of the working class either in Britain or in 'oppressed nations' and focused more specifically on the issue of civil rights for all, demanding the end to unemployment and the need for equal pay. The programme was worthy but not revolutionary.[6]

Today, even such acknowledgements of the condition of the people of the Global South are increasingly difficult to come by. Modern antiracism seems to mirror the Faustian pact that Black Power radicals had indicted the 'white left' for many decades ago; of the drive for social advances at home and silence on the question of imperialism abroad.

Where this shift inwards towards a civic antiracist politics did not happen naturally, it was coerced by the state. The instinctive pan-Muslim solidarity for the *ummah* that shaped Muslim opposition to the 'War on Terror' was pathologised as signs of proto-terrorist 'extremism' among individuals, who were then subject to surveillance and tests of loyalty to 'British Values'. Meanwhile under early iterations of the 'Prevent' strategy, Muslim organisations born of the rib of the British government served to ventriloquise government policy to Muslims and try to draw their attention towards homegrown issues rather than matters of foreign policy, and since the 7/7 attacks all manner of organisations have sought to manufacture 'well-integrated' and civic-minded British Muslims.

6 Anandi Ramamurthy, *Black Star: Britain's Asian Youth Movements* (London: Pluto Press, 2013), p. 187.

Ultimately, the state strategy of inclusion allowed British state racism to reinforce its structuring logic: the division between *natives* and citizens who could lend their consent to a political system predicated on the exploitation of *aliens* and outsiders. This duality is embodied by the trade-off between anti-discrimination race relations laws being passed almost concurrent with anti-immigration laws during the 1960s.

But the indigenisation of Black and brown politics over the course of the 1980s would not change the fact that domestic British racism remains intrinsically connected to Britain's evolving position in the international system. From the Arabs facing internment in Britain during the Gulf War, to the Third World asylum seeker excluded by the borders of the then-new European Union – British state racism of the 1990s and beyond would be defined, as ever, against the foreigner and the non-citizen. The Third World asylum seeker soon blurred into the 'radical preacher' and 'Muslim extremist' with the onset of the War on Terror, while ostensibly 'white' Eastern Europeans on the EU's peripheries were soon the subject of vicious xenophobia in the new millennium. As long as Britain remains embedded in a global hierarchy of states, antiracists here can never ignore the international impact of British politics – because sooner or later, it always comes knocking on Britain's door.

Internationalism against imperialism

The internationalism of the Black Power era waned as the Third World revolt from which it took inspiration spiralled into decline; the retreat of the domestic forces of progress mirroring the defeat of the Third World bloc during the Reagan-Thatcher era.

Despite this, it is difficult to claim that internationalism per se has been lost. In this era of globalisation and hyper-connected social media, it is near impossible for any movement to remain hermetically sealed off from the outside – not least in places like Britain. The worldwide Black Lives Matter explosion, after all, found its inspiration from the example of the US. But what this long period of decline achieved was to disrupt the circuitry of radical internationalism that prevailed in the previous era, and distort the meaning of 'internationalism'. Recovering a radical internationalism demands that we reject a literalist, depoliticised understanding of the term. Internationalism is a politically diverse set of politics, like any other – not all internationalisms are alike, not all internationalisms are uniformly positive. And to be certain, not all internationalisms are anti-imperialist internationalisms in the vein of Black Power. Theirs was defined by its vision of a unity of people's struggles for land and liberation, and by its attentiveness to the international division of labour, of wealth and of humanity – which if not reducible to racism, was indelibly marked by it.

On the other hand, at the turn of the twentieth century, future Labour Prime Minister Ramsey MacDonald defined the British Empire as an exercise in internationalism par excellence. In his words, 'The [British] Empire must exist not merely for safety, or order, or peace, but for richness of life'[7] and that 'To its subject races [the Labour party] desires to occupy the position of friend'.[8] Closer to the modern day, US President Joe Biden framed his successful electoral campaign around a 'return' to an American 'internationalist' tradition that strives for global leadership, as opposed to the supposed 'isolationism' of Donald Trump. These were words that would strike a very different chord across the Global South – for whom this is an interna-

7 James Ramsay MacDonald, *Labour and the Empire* (London: G. Allen, 1907), p. 49.
8 Ibid., p. 107.

tionalist tradition embedded in military bases on their shores, advanced at the barrel of a gun, and imprinted in the shattered bodies and minds of millions of people across the globe.

And yet, today we are trapped in a suffocating binary whereby internationalism is framed as an indisputable good, in contrast to short-sighted and regressive nationalism. This has been the terms of debate around Brexit, where the predominant narratives have rested on supposedly cosmopolitan Europhiles struggling for the soul of Britain against atavistic 'little Englander' nationalists. But this binary framing blurs into incoherence. To blithely equivocate between the nationalism of the British National Party with that of, say, Cuban revolutionaries would reflect a fundamental unseriousness about questions of power, history and the task of human emancipation. This binary also elides the question of just who and what is best served by any given form of internationalism. In the context of Brexit, it erases the extraordinary violence inflicted by the European Union and its *Fortress Europe* policies on immigrants and refugees, which has turned the Mediterranean sea into a clear blue killing field. It also ignores the fact that the EU is, at heart, an irredeemably imperialist formation: helping drain wealth from the Global South and its own peripheral states, enriching the states of Western Europe, and buffering the Union from the 'dark hordes' of Africa and Asia fleeing desperate lives for it. The burial shroud of the EU flag is no more worthy of affection than the Butcher's Apron of the Union Jack.

Whatever 'internationalism' one adheres to, then, must be born of the recognition we live in a world stratified by imperialism and its institutions. Internationalism does not exist on neutral terrain, but operates either in relation, in acquiescence with, or in opposition to imperialist rule. An internationalism that confines itself to upholding abstract values without considering the institutions that enforce them, or the power structure in which those values are mobilised, is ripe for disaster. This is none more urgent at a time when internationalism is often approached through the framework of 'human rights'.

In the name of human rights

This chapter was being put together in the midst of the United States and its allies' inglorious retreat from their two decade-long occupation of Afghanistan. Initiated following the 9/11 attacks, the war and subsequent occupation was legitimised by influential figureheads in the West as a struggle for 'freedom', for 'human rights' – and most damningly as a 'feminist invasion', a means to advance the rights of Afghan women who had lived under the Taliban.

But what becomes of a feminism such as this, prosecuted with imperial zeal? The war was one in which hundreds of thousands of Afghans were killed and millions more left impoverished, into which trillions of dollars were sunk for the benefit of arms companies, and which – through the broader 'War on Terror' framework – paved the way for states across the Global South to become zones of devastation and dispossession. This jarring juxtaposition – of seemingly high-minded values legitimising horrific violence – is of critical importance today, when a human rights internationalism is the pre-eminent means through which 'internationalist' politics are negotiated. This is even more pressing when international human rights NGOs often serve as windows into affairs in the Global South for those of us in the Global North.

Modern human rights internationalism matured almost in tandem with the rise of Thatcherism-Reaganism, as radical Third

World governments were forced to once again bend the knee to the West. This was followed by the proliferation of human rights NGOs/iNGOs such as Human Rights Watch, with international institutions like the Ford Foundation and now Google pouring funding into those countries to sweep activists off the streets and into NGOs. As with domestic Antiracism from Above, so with internationalism: this NGOisation of human rights internationalism has displaced the mass parties, radical governments and democratic peoples' struggles that had been the motors of change at home and abroad before it. In its place, internationalism became mediated through a global consortium of NGOs/iNGOs themselves often deeply entangled with Western governments and institutions like the EU and UN. The connection between radical groups in Britain with radical movements and parties in the Global South was broken, and internationalism was re-routed through these professionalised forums, taking on a more elitist character. This human rights internationalism has also had a vexed relationship with the socialist, anti-imperialist and labour internationalisms that had flowered in the decades prior. Steve Striffler summarises this tension in his book *Solidarity*, as one whereby

> A contracted political horizon, generated in part by the decline of the left, helped produce the human rights movement, but the human rights movement also made it more difficult to imagine and pursue more revolutionary forms of internationalism.[9]

But perhaps most problematic is how regularly it ends up promoting an internationalism that erases questions of imperialism

9 Steve Striffler, *Solidarity: Latin America and the US Left in the Era of Human Rights* (London: Pluto, 2019).

from the equation, and instead appeals to the authority of those institutions in which imperialism is enshrined: the US government, NATO, the IMF and others.

This erasure plays out in three interrelated sleight-of-hand when it comes to the approach of many iNGOs to struggles rooted in the Global South. Firstly, human rights internationalism dislocates social struggles from history – by personalising social problems within individual politicians or 'regimes', while evading more complex legacies of colonialism or imperial domination. Then it cleaves apart social and political rights from the issue of economic justice that grounds them – such that battles over the ballot are given far greater currency than basic demands for bread and housing. And finally it decouples rights and democracy from the material bases that make them possible. No longer is the emphasis placed on local self-determination, or struggles for national sovereignty, but rather rights and democracy are rewritten as things that can be imposed externally by iNGOs in the Global North, institutions like the World Bank – or Western militaries. It is in this way that human rights can become summoned up in service of imperialism – as in Afghanistan, and numerous other zones across the world. And by operating under the pretence of internationalism, this approach allows people in the West to project their own prejudices onto the national struggles of people in the Global South, while trafficking in racist tropes of foreign 'despots' and 'authoritarians'.

In 1954 William Worthy denounced the deployment of Blacks in America's war on Korea, firing a prescient warning shot against those who saw an inclusive US imperialism as offering Blacks any promise on the home front. Almost 70 years later, US President Joe Biden unveiled a renewed 'diversity drive' across the military and federal institutions,[10] as part of his attempt to manage the mass social contradictions spilling out at home, in order to stave off declining US prestige worldwide. The very fact that particular forms of feminism or human rights have allowed themselves to be used in service of hegemonic power speaks to their own patterns of co-option and containment. The emergence of 'green' justifications for war should be at the forefront of any radical climate justice agenda. The none-too-outlandish thought of 'antiracist' internationalism being used to further the interests of British or US imperialism should give us serious pause for thought.

Palestine

Nowhere is the 'contracted political horizon' of human rights more evident today than in the case of Palestine. It is where the many competing internationalisms come to nest, and where the contradictions between them come to a head.

The question of Palestine is, and has historically been, a linchpin of liberatory politics. Despite having their own aspirations denied, the Palestinian national liberation struggle has electrified revolutionary movements worldwide – from Black internationalists, Third World struggles, Pan Arabists and socialists – and has been central to how they knit together their understanding of the world. On the other hand, it has also sparked a deeply reactionary counter-internationalism, with right-wing governments, fascist movements, war-hawks and security industries colluding in defence of Israel, and investing in the ongoing dispossession of Palestinians. Israel's role as force

10 https://defense.gov/News/News-Stories/Article/Article/2529262/biden-showcases-the-strength-excellence-of-american-military-diversity (last accessed August 2021).

multiplier for imperialism in the 'Middle East' has cemented an unholy alliance between it and states as diverse as the fellow settler colonies of the US and Australia, the ultra-reactionaries of Saudi Arabia and Viktor Orbán's Hungary, and the quasi-fascism of Jair Bolsonaro's Brazil and Narendra Modi's India.

Support for the Palestinian liberation struggle is a clear political line of demarcation. But equally important is precisely how (and how far) one extends that support. At root it is a struggle that integrates multiple axes of violence, from settler colonialism[11] to imperialism to state violence to racism to labour struggles and more – and any attempt to pry these apart serves to distort it. One cannot understand Israel's deep rooted anti-Palestinian racism without considering the settler colonial project that this racism legitimises; one cannot understand that settler colonial project without considering Israel's role as an outpost of Western imperialism in the region, and so forth.

But the redefinition of Palestine as solely or predominantly a humanitarian cause has attempted to do just this – whereby the political and historical contours of the struggle are flattened into yet another human rights issue to jostle for attention spans in a world of infinite injustices. Integral questions such as the right of return for exiled Palestinians are jettisoned in favour of a simple moral opposition to the 'excesses' of Israeli state violence, or its settlements in isolation. And the locus of the struggle is moved from Palestinian resistance to salaried human rights advocates. This is in turn illustrated in the perverse tendency of international human rights organisations and certain Western commentators, to police the terms of the Palestinians' struggle – to temper their aspirations in order to indulge the consciences of the 'international community'. We see this also in the deeply

11 https://bdsmovement.net/colonialism-and-apartheid/settler-colonialism (last accessed August 2021).

racist way that Palestinians are expected to perform their right to humanity before the world through a ritualistic devotion to pacifism, and in the censure reserved for Palestinian resistance movements by NGOs which place their actions on a par with the brutality of the Israeli regime.

And finally, as humanitarian campaigns rely on clean and uncomplicated protagonists and antagonists to rally their supporters, their 'benefactors' are consigned to a cycle of virtuous suffering – with Palestinian life seemingly only becoming valuable in death.

Disciplining radical internationalism

The example of Palestine is also central to an analysis of radical internationalism because of the way it has served as a petri dish for the many disciplining strategies designed to suffocate radical internationalism today.

The vilification of the Palestinian national liberation struggle and its movements as 'terrorists' long precedes the twenty-first century's 'War on Terror' – Deepa Kumar argues that in fact Israeli security forces helped circulate the notion of Arab terrorists to the US in the aftermath of the 1967 Six Day War.[12] But the emergence of that war was a boon for Israel, allowing it to recast its effort to dispossess the Palestinians as a struggle against 'terrorists' that demanded international support, while also tapping into a wellspring of Islamophobia. In the last two decades, the many tactics and technologies of countering 'terrorism' have been used to brutally repress Palestinian resistance, and suppress expressions of international solidarity with them.

---

12 *Empire, Islamophobia and the War on Terror* [Webinar] Transnational Institute, 2021, available at: https://tni.org/en/article/empire-islamophobia-and-the-war-on-terror (last accessed September 2021).

Effective US monopoly control on international finance flows can make its formal designation of liberation movements as 'terrorist' fatal – paving the way for sanctions and asset freezes, crushing those movements and cutting them off from international support. The case of the 'Holy Land Five' stands as a bleak testament to this War on Terror-era climate, with five Palestinian-American charity leaders convicted on the spurious charge of providing 'material support to terrorists', and languishing in prison for a combined sentence of nearly 200 years.

Palestine solidarity has also been subject to fierce online surveillance and censorship, with pro-Palestine content regularly leading to censorship, account suspensions and flagged posts on platforms like Twitter and Facebook. In 2016, Israel's justice minister Ayelet Shaked boasted that Facebook, Google and YouTube were 'complying with up to 95 percent of Israeli requests to delete content, almost all of it Palestinian' on the grounds of 'incitement'.[13]

The Anti-Defamation League, a pro-Israel lobby group with a 'long history of surveillance of social justice movements, including civil rights, anti-Apartheid, immigrant, farmworker, queer, Palestinian rights, and labor movements'[14] established a 'command centre' in Silicon Valley in 2017 to monitor what it termed 'online hate speech'.[15] That same year, it was appointed

---

13 https://middleeasteye.net/opinion/palestine-facebook-twitter-google-erasure-warning (last accessed August 2021).

14 https://droptheadl.org/the-adl-is-not-an-ally/#palestinian-rights (last accessed August 2021). See also Akhil Gopal & Celine Qussiny, 'Zionist Instrumentalization of the Global War on Terror', *The Terror Trap The Impact of the War on Terror on Muslim Communities Since 9/11*, https://bridge.georgetown.edu/research/the-terror-trap-the-impact-of-the-war-on-terror-on-muslim-communities-since-9-11 and https://latimes.com/archives/la-xpm-1993-04-13-mn-22383-story.html (last accessed August 2021).

15 https://time.com/4699823/adl-silicon-valley-hate-center (last accessed August 2021).

a trusted flagger organisation for YouTube, meaning its reporting of content for removal was prioritised.[16] During the COVID pandemic, when video conferences became the new standard, Zoom blocked the software being used to host Popular Front for the Liberation of Palestine icon Leila Khaled at multiple events.

Recent years have also seen a concerted attempt to thwart the growing public solidarity for Palestinians through the force of domestic law, hemming in the terms of this solidarity and insulating Israel from critique. Litigious 'lawfare' strategies by pro-Israel advocates, designed to frustrate and criminalise Boycott, Divestment and Sanctions (BDS) campaigns, have become scorched earth campaigns that threaten to undermine civil freedoms, political organisations and democracy itself.[17]

The forceful codification of the International Holocaust Remembrance Alliance (IHRA) definition of anti-Semitism has been central to this project of delegitimising internationalism. By weaving it into governing policies of the British government, public institutions and political parties, even milquetoast expressions of support for Palestine have been subject to censure, while meaningful critiques of Zionism, settler colonialism or the failed 'two state' paradigm are rendered 'anti-Semitic'.[18] The expansion of the IHRA definition forms part of an effort to redefine anti-Zionism as anti-Semitism, to make Palestine synonymous with the issue of 'hate crime', and to collapse Palestine solidarity into the sphere of policing and security. This sleight of hand is designed to police the question of Palestine out of sight

---

16 https://adl.org/news/press-releases/adl-applauds-google-and-youtube-in-expanding-initiative-to-fight-online-hate (last accessed August 2021).

17 https://tni.org/en/publication/shrinking-space-and-the-bds-movement (last accessed August 2021).

18 https://theguardian.com/news/2020/nov/29/palestinian-rights-and-the-ihra-definition-of-antisemitism (last accessed August 2021).

and out of mind, with bad faith manipulations of language at the thin end of the wedge opening out to an assault on any expressions of Palestine solidarity.

Most perversely, it has enabled arch-reactionaries of British society – the hate-scribes of the British tabloids, the most repugnant elements of the political class – to masquerade as 'antiracist' militants in the public eye. It has allowed figures to legitimise their barely veiled disdain for Palestinian life by targeting pro-Palestine activists as 'racists', dredging up their social media posts and intimate personal details for public consumption, and hounding them out of livelihoods and into silence. And in doing so, the policing of Palestine solidarity has served as a stick to bludgeon anti-imperialist and left politics more broadly.

This last point represents the logical endpoint of antiracist campaigns that centre on legalism and procedural approaches that we have critiqued in Chapter 5. The practice of uprooting racism from a *structural* analysis, and placing it into the realm of *process*, paves the way for the decoupling of antiracism from the imperatives of anti-imperialism. And finally, what the policing of discourse and activism around Palestine represents is an 'antiracism' in service of empire, and intersecting with the interests of power. It represents the very antithesis of the radical internationalism represented in the era of Black Power in Britain – but perhaps most tellingly, it reflects the dangers of an 'antiracism' that makes peace with the prevailing climate of law and order that is increasingly coming to define British society.

Chapter 8

Policing and surveillance today

Law and order Britain

The racist politics of law and order have been central to the institutional reorganisation of Britain, with a slew of laws being pushed through since the 2019 General Election alone. These include the draconian Police, Crime, Sentencing and Courts Bill, introduced following the 2020 protests, which heralds a stark crackdown on protest rights, a mass expansion of policing techniques and technologies throughout society. It is couched in explicitly racist motivations such as its proposed criminalisation of Gypsy, Roma and Travellers' (GRT) ways of life.

Just prior to this bill came the Covert Human Intelligence Sources (Criminal Conduct) Act, giving a free hand to undercover agents to engage in all manner of crimes against the public in the course of their work. Meanwhile, the Overseas Operations Act insulated British soldiers and the Ministry of Defence from prosecutions for the brutality that they commit in the name of the British state abroad. Moreover, the socialising of policing – by drawing the public into the work of spotting 'terrorists', scouting for 'illegal' immigrants or informing on 'benefit cheats' – has embedded this law and order within Britain's cultural world, qualitatively expanding the realm of policing.

This latest law and order approach is not simply a matter of policing for policing's sake, but forms part of a firmer realignment between political institutions and policing. As the British state retreats ever further from social provisions, the only language it speaks is violence. And in order to insulate the state from popular pressure, the government requires the loyalty of its coercive forces. Home Secretary Priti Patel's speech to the Police Federation in June 2021 put this in plainer terms than we ever could, when she told them bluntly that 'I am your political advocate in Westminster.'[1]

And yet, strategies to counter the proliferation of law and order policies have not moved as swiftly with the times. The strategy of community patronage continues to be utilised by police forces across the country, keeping communities sated with promise of reviews and reports, while racist policing remains the reality on the streets.

After meeting the families of Olaseni 'Seni' Lewis and Sean Rigg in January 2015, then-Home Secretary Theresa May commissioned the Angiolini Review into Deaths in Police Custody.[2] During the ten months in which the report was being compiled, the death toll of British policing mounted – including the killings of Rashan Charles and Edwin De Costa in London. The Angiolini report was kicked into the long grass after its publication, with several groups supporting families impacted by deaths in custody calling for its recommendations to be implemented.

The pacifying effect of reviews and community policing was well understood by the Brixton Defence Campaign, set up to defend the huge numbers arrested in the aftermath of the 1981

1 https://gov.uk/government/speeches/home-secretary-at-the-police-federation-conference-2021 (last accessed September 2021).

2 https://gov.uk/government/publications/deaths-and-serious-incidents-in-police-custody (last accessed September 2021).

Brixton uprising – which encouraged people to boycott the Scarman Inquiry. As recorded by *Race & Class*, the group stated that the inquiry will only 'provide justification *for* dramatically increasing repressiveness in policing methods which are already massively racist, lawless and brutal.'[3]

Similarly, after the uprising in Moss Side in 1981, and after being subject to Anderton's policing response, the Moss Side Defence Committee called for a boycott of the Hytner Inquiry, set up to learn the local lessons of the riots. Like their comrades in Brixton, the locals understood the 'thin veneer of liberalism' these reports provided to violent policing and this section of their report is worth quoting at length:

> The Defence Committee sees the Hytner Inquiry as:
> - Riddled with inconsistencies
> - Suffused with condescending ignorance about the people of Moss Side and particularly about its Black population
> - Deeply biased in its identification of the cause of the riots
> - Evasive of all issues which the people of Moss Side would see as central and decisive, and in its comments and recommendations
> - Blatantly concerned to conceal those issues behind a facade of cosmetic operations designed to reconcile the people of Moss Side to a form of policing that which would remain substantially unchanged[4]

Reading the statements from the Moss Side Defence Committee and Brixton Defence Campaign, we can see resistance to the

3 'The "riots"', *Race & Class*, 23:2–3, (October 1981), pp. 223–32.

4 'The Hytner Inquiry – A preliminary critique of the report by Ben Hytner QC on the disturbances in Moss Side, Manchester, on 8/9 July 1981' by the Moss Side Defence Committee, quoted in Gus John, *Moss Side 1981: More than just a riot* (London: New Beacon Books, 2011), p. 5.

tendrils of containment introduced by those seeking to manage dissent and rebellion. With the new political climate developing, some policing figures have even been emboldened to drop their 'community relations' facade entirely. Four decades after James Anderton's reign as Greater Manchester Chief Constable, his present-day successor Stephen Watson began his term by going head-to-head with the chair of the Greater Manchester Race Equality Panel, denying the existence of institutional racism in the force and suggesting they simply recruit a more diverse pool of officers.[5] It is clear that we cannot continue to recycle a failed formula, when even those in positions of power are no longer interested in maintaining any illusions about it.

Community-police partnership panels and community scrutiny panels offer the public the scantest of information, projecting a veneer of collaboration and progress as deaths in custody continue to pile up. These panels in turn provide a patina of authenticity to police statements whenever community anger towards policing begins to rise. But this cycle is slowly coming undone.

2011

'Well, Wha wha wha what's your name then son?'
My name Smiley Culture
'Yeah, Where do you think you're coming from lad?'
From seeing me mother
'What's the registration number of the car then?'
I can't remember
'What you got in the boot then son?'
A cassette recorder. Would you like to have a look?
'Shut your bloody mouth. We ask. You answer

5 https://theguardian.com/uk-news/2021/jul/27/manchester-police-chief-rejects-claim-of-institutional-racism (last accessed September 2021).

Now take the keys out of the car and step out of the motor
Me and my colleagues have got a few questions to ask ya
You'll be on your way as soon as we get an answer

'Police Officer' – Smiley Culture, 1984

The New Labour governments of Tony Blair and Gordon Brown had unleashed a dramatic expansion of British policing. During the first nine years of Tony Blair's administration, his government had created, on average, a new offence for each day in office.[6]

Despite presiding over the Macpherson inquiry discussed in Chapter 4, the Labour government had begun rolling back its diagnosis of institutional racism in the Met as soon as politically possible. In 2003, Home Secretary David Blunkett expressed his concern to colleagues that 'the slogan created a year or two ago about institutional racism missed the point',[7] and days away from the ten year anniversary of the Macpherson report, Justice Secretary Jack Straw denied that the charge of institutional racism still held true.[8] Britain's brief 'reckoning' with institutional racism also coincided with the passage of anti-asylum seeker immigration laws under the Labour governments, and the development of an extraordinarily vast domestic surveillance apparatus honed in on Muslims in Britain under the banner of 'countering terrorism'.[9] In the

6 https://independent.co.uk/news/uk/politics/blair-s-frenzied-law-making-a-new-offence-for-every-day-spent-in-office-412072.html (last accessed September 2021).

7 https://theguardian.com/politics/2003/jan/14/immigrationpolicy.race (last accessed September 2021).

8 https://theguardian.com/politics/2009/feb/23/met-police-racism (last accessed September 2021).

9 For more on the Labour government's record on immigration, asylum and counterterrorism, see Arun Kundnani, *The End of Tolerance: Racism in 21st Century Britain*, (London: Pluto, 2007).

middle of this, by 2008 then-PM Gordon Brown and future PM David Cameron engaged in a Dutch auction on police powers, each of them pledging to grant police license to stop and search individuals without suspicion.[10] Dismissing allegations that these amounted to a return to the Sus laws that helped spark the 1981 rebellions, Cameron claimed that these concerns were relics of the past: according to him, Britain's police were no longer racist.[11]

In March 2011, David Victor Emmanuel, better known by his artist name Smiley Culture, died under very suspicious circumstances during a police search of his home in Surrey. Twelve days later in North Birmingham, Kingsley Burrell called the police for help while out with his son, reporting being followed by some men. Upon being detained under the Mental Health Act by officers suspecting a mental health episode, Kingsley was handcuffed, brutalised and left face down in a hospital secure room with a blanket over his head.[12] He died following a cardiac arrest days later. A mere two months after that, Demetre Fraser fell from the eleventh floor of a tower block in South Birmingham, in the middle of a struggle with visiting police officers.[13] This string of Black deaths in police custody would set the tone for an exceptionally hot summer in Britain, with youth already feeling the impact of the new coalition government's austerity agenda, and its scrapping of education support grants.

---

10 http://news.bbc.co.uk/1/hi/uk_politics/7216815.stm (last accessed September 2021).

11 Ibid.

12 To find out more about the case of Kingsley Burrell, see: https://4wardeveruk.org/cases/adult-cases-uk/police-medical-asylum/kingsley-burrell (last accessed September 2021).

13 To find out more about the case of Demetre Fraser, see: https://4wardeveruk.org/cases/youth-cases-uk/police-restraint/demetre-fraser (last accessed September 2021).

Tottenham was the spark. On 4 August, news began to emerge that the police had killed Mark Duggan in Tottenham Hale. Initial details were clouded by police disinformation, with the police accountability body the IPCC (Independent Police Complaints Commission, since replaced by the IOPC, Independent Office for Police Conduct) releasing a statement falsely claiming a two-way shootout between police and Duggan. After having been uncritically circulated by the media, the claim was retracted: the only bullets fired had been from the police.

Two days later, Duggan's family and the Tottenham community marched from the Broadwater Farm estate to Tottenham Police Station to demand a response from a senior officer. Following a violent police response, with a woman being struck by a police officer, a brick was thrown through the window of an unattended police car.

Tottenham erupted.

By the next day the flames licked across London North, South, East and West. Over the course of five hot days in summer 2011, Britain witnessed the largest revolts against police since 1981, with youth confronting police across Birmingham, Manchester, Bristol, Nottingham, Leeds and far beyond – spanning 66 localities in total.

Prime Minister David Cameron denied any political motivation to the revolts, dismissing it as a symbol of 'moral collapse', poor parenting and criminality.[14] And unlike his predecessor three decades prior, Cameron did not initiate a public inquiry. To add final insult to injury, that year the annual United Friends and Family Campaign (UFFC) procession, held by families and friends of those killed in custody, was attacked by police[15] – with

14 https://bbc.co.uk/news/uk-politics-14524834 (last accessed September 2021).

15 https://ceasefiremagazine.co.uk/breaking-news-deaths-custody-march-attacked-police (last accessed September 2021).

the moving memorial of mothers, fathers, siblings and partners violently interrupted by officers.

Growing arsenal

Let it go down in history
The word is that officially
She died democratically
In 13 feet of tape,
That Christian was over here
Because pirates were over there
The Bible sent us everywhere
To make Great Britain great.
Here lies the extradition squad
And we should all now pray to God
That as they go about their job
They make not one mistake,
For I fear as I walk the streets
That one day I just may meet
Officials who may tie my feet
And how would I escape.

'The Death of Joy Gardner' – Benjamin Zephaniah

The state response was vicious.

A lesson had to be taught: it was not enough to lock up the youth; the community would have to pay a price too. The government needed to ensure that kids who witnessed police fleeing from their peers would never dare to challenge police authority in the coming years. Raids became an everyday reality for the communities who rose against the police, with over 3,000 being arrested following the revolts. Eviction proceedings were moved against families of individuals participating in the rebellions who were living in public housing.[16] The British public were recruited into the work of policing, with images of suspects beamed across giant screens in cities like Manchester and Salford to encourage them to identify community members for arrest.

Then came the Gangs Matrix.

In the days following the revolts, Mayor of London Boris Johnson declared it was time to deal with 'gangs', with David Cameron declaring an all-out war on gangs and 'gang culture'. The Gangs Matrix formed part of this response, with swathes of young, primarily Black and almost exclusively men placed into a police database effectively for their supposed proximity to criminality – including being a victim of crime themselves. Being placed on the Matrix put them at risk of ongoing surveillance, having data shared on them between sectors, and having driving license applications denied – despite 64% of those on the Matrix never committing any offences. Data showed that Black men made up 78% of the names on the Matrix, massively out of sync with the demographics involved in youth violence.[17]

A report released in May 2020 by Amnesty international showed that sharing of Youtube videos, or referencing supposed 'gang'-related colours – alongside other spurious pieces of intelligence – was used as evidence to place someone on the Matrix. Officers were even known to create fake social media accounts to follow or send friend requests in order to gauge further information, forgoing the need to obtain a warrant for such intimate surveillance. The Information Commissioner's Office was

16 https://theguardian.com/uk/2011/aug/12/london-riots-wandsworth-council-eviction (last accessed September 2021).

17 https://amnesty.org.uk/london-trident-gangs-matrix-metropolitan-police (last accessed September 2021).

forced to issue the Met with a formal enforcement to improve the guidance around the Matrix and apply proportionality in its usage and sharing. Subsequently, hundreds have been removed from the Matrix. Yet the Matrix is still in operation, and there appears to be no end in sight to policing today.

Over the last decade, policing in Britain has undergone a large expansion in other fields too. One of the emerging areas of expansion is in the introduction of school-based police officers, following the approach taken across the Atlantic. This entrenches surveillance within schools and exposes ever-younger groups of people to the threat of police violence. In Manchester, the Northern Police Monitoring Project and Kids of Colour created the *No Police in Schools Campaign*[18] collecting testimonials from young people, teachers, parents and community members to resist the introduction of school officers – though as of the time of writing – they remain at a borough wide level. The campaign continues to call for more investment in pastoral support and the complete removal of police from schools – while elected representatives like London Mayor Sadiq Khan have called for increased police presence in schools.

As the role of policing in society has expanded, so too has the arsenal of tools now at their disposal. Armed police officers are becoming an increasingly common presence at even small protests, while rows of riot police lined the streets during Black Lives Matters protests in summer 2020. Taser usage has gone up by over 500% in the last decade.[19] Some forces such as Northamptonshire Police Force have equipped every front-

18 To find out more on the No Police in Schools Campaigns, visit: https://nopoliceinschools.co.uk (last accessed).

19 Resistance Lab, 'Despite their claims to the contrary, Taser usage by Greater Manchester Police has risen to its highest ever level (Manchester, 2021), retrieved from: resistancelab.network/ (last accessed).

line officer with a taser[20] – this in a council that had declared bankruptcy in 2018, and reduced its services to skeletal levels. Despite the growing number of taser-related deaths at the hands of the police, there was a 78% increase in the use of tasers against children under 18 in 2018/19 compared to the year prior, with 29 incidents involving children under eleven.[21]

Increasingly under scrutiny too are the growing number of fatalities in police pursuits or police vehicle-related deaths. In Toxteth 1981, the police used land rovers to ram into protestors – the first victim Paul Conroy, a white youth, had his back broken and soon after David Moore, a disabled white youth was killed by a police van.[22] Over the last few years there have been a growing number of deaths involving police vehicles including in police pursuits or after police vehicles drive dangerously, such as the tragic case of 22-year-old Jade Mutua who was waiting for her boyfriend when she was killed by a Metropolitan Police car driving at twice the speed limit.

In 2017, the Policing Minister Nick Hurd commissioned a review and consultation around police pursuits. The consultation – of which nearly 60% of respondents were from the police themselves – called for greater impunity for police during pursuits, and for them to be considered to a different standard to public drivers.[23] In late 2018, then-Home Secretary Sajid

20 https://northants.police.uk/news/northants/news/news/2019/august-19/northamptonshire-police-is-the-first-police-force-in-the-country-to-arm-all-frontline-officers-with-tasers/ (last accessed September 2021).

21 UK Home Office, 'Police use of force statistics, England and Wales: April 2018 to March 2019', (19 December 2019), https://assets.publishing.service.gov.uk/government/uploads/system/uploads/attachment_data/file/853204/police-use-of-force-apr2018-mar2019-hosb3319.pdf (last accessed December 2021).

22 'The "riots"', *Race & Class*, 23:2–3, (October 1981), p. 228.

23 https://gov.uk/government/consultations/police-pursuits/outcome/the-law-guidance-and-training-governing-police-pursuits-government-response-accessible-version (last accessed September 2021).

Javid publicly declared support for the tactic of police drivers ramming suspects off their mopeds during police pursuits.[24] In 2019, deaths during police pursuits reached a 13-year high.[25]

Surveillance

You cannot say that you're preventing terrorists
If all that you're doing is pre-empting terrorists
Perhaps if instead of Prevent we could ponder the past that made political violence probable
But imperialism loves to pretend itself away
So police are given more powers as if policing protects the nation
And prisons and deportation plans are methods of purgation
In the end Prevent is nothing but political deflection
Proof that the state is headed in the most authoritarian direction
So prepare for permanent conditions of political persecution
'Cos even if it's not yet palpable to you
The project of resistance if your obligation, too
The project of resistance is your obligation, too

'P P P Prevent' – Suhaiymah Manzoor Khan

The Spycops Inquiry, discussed in Chapter 2, and the declassification of police documents have exposed the network of surveillance that faced left-wing, working-class and antiracist campaigns across the country following the formation of the

24 https://news.sky.com/story/home-secretary-sajid-javid-backs-police-knocking-suspects-off-mopeds-11565876 (last accessed September 2021).

25 https://theguardian.com/uk-news/2019/sep/05/number-road-deaths-involving-police-vehicles-13-year-high (last accessed September 2021).

'Spycops' divisions in 1968.[26] The scope of groups facing surveillance has included 18 of the families campaigning for justice after deaths at the hand of racism and death at the hands of the state[27] – including the relatives of Cherry Groce whose shooting by police sparked the 1985 Brixton riots, the families of Stephen Lawrence, Michael Menson and Ricky Reel – three young men killed by racists during the 1990s – and all the way to the family of Jean Charles de Menezes.

The turn of the century saw a qualitative shift in the state of surveillance in Britain. In summer 2000, the breathtakingly broad Terrorism Act (2000) passed through Parliament, introduced by the Labour Home Secretary Jack Straw – who opened the debate with a deeply ironic ode to the importance of protecting essential freedoms. The 9/11 attacks and the onset of the 'War on Terror' a year later brought with it a raft of legislation, granting the British state historically unprecedented levels of power of surveillance, policing and coercion. In the context of Britain's military pursuits across the Global South, these policies allowed for domestic dissent to be recast as nascent forms of 'terrorism' or 'extremism' open to heavy sanction – while simultaneously allowing Britain's imperial might to be wielded with minimal scrutiny.

The Terrorism Act (2000) provided the legislative backbone of further 'counterterror' laws post-2001, and would be the first of many which would see our freedoms eroded and the powers of the state ratcheted ever upwards. These have included the Anti-Terrorism, Crime and Security Act 2001, Terrorism Act 2006, Terrorism Prevention and Investigative Measures

26 https://theguardian.com/uk-news/2018/oct/15/undercover-police-spies-infiltrated-uk-leftwing-groups-for-decades (last accessed September 2021).

27 https://theguardian.com/commentisfree/2019/oct/25/police-spied-grieving-black-families (last accessed September 2021).

Act 2011, Counter-Terrorism and Security Act 2015 and the Counter-Terrorism and Border Security Act 2019. This swathe of 'counterterror' legislation would see, among other concerns, the inversion of criminal justice norms, the expansion of surveillance apparatus and increased powers of deportation and detention. Stretching across New Labour, the coalition government through to the Conservative governments, wave after wave of legislation would be introduced with relative ease given the almost unbroken consensus on the War on Terror across political parties.

But beyond the force of law, the ethos of 'counterterror' surveillance took on a life of its own as a cultural project, reproduced through daily interactions; a climate of mutual suspicion reflecting the insecurity of our current times. The 'Prevent' programme has emerged as possibly the most symbolic of this counterterror cultural project. Publicly introduced by New Labour in 2006, it forms one part of the government's Counter-terrorism Strategy, and operates in what the government terms the 'pre-criminal space'. Aiming to identify those who would be vulnerable to so-called 'extremist' ideology, the strategy has expanded the realm of policing across society, while undermining relationships of trust and care in classrooms, hospital rooms and settings across the country.

Of the many thousands of referrals made every year, a small handful register in the public consciousness – Muslim children referred for wearing t-shirts with Arabic names, expressing the slightest support for Palestine or simply repeating things they learned in school. As time has gone on, Black Lives Matter, Extinction Rebellion and other groups associated with social change have appeared across Prevent and/or counterterrorism literature, as policing agencies attempt to intimidate the youth into subservience. At heart, Prevent has always been a project of breaking down social relations and bonds of solidarity, and securitising them – isolating and repressing dissent and creating a 'chilling effect' across all areas of public life. After being made a statutory duty in the Counter-terrorism and Security Act 2015, the proportion of young people being referred for investigation to Prevent has exploded. In a familiar pattern, young people are being exposed to the realities of state violence earlier and earlier, in a bid to engineer their silence and compliance as they mature into a world riddled with injustice.

Since its inception, Prevent has operated like a highly-securitised form of the 'community-police' model expanded after 1981, resting on a carefully curated system of engagement and isolation with predominantly Muslim organisations. Many Muslim organisations had become entangled with the programme in some form or another, with Prevent grants often filling in for shortfalls in local government funding after the onset of austerity, thereby extending the tendrils of Prevent into communities across the country.

A growing chasm

The mix of intimidation, acquiescence, consent that the Prevent programme had relied on has begun to unravel in recent years. Successive Conservative governments since 2010 have gradually dispensed with their attempts to maintain some measure of consent from Muslims, instead opting for more overt coercion.

The last straw seems to have broken with the Johnson government's handling of an 'Independent Review' of Prevent, appended at the last minute to the Counter-Terrorism and Border Security Act 2019 as it made its way through Parliament, following demands from human rights NGOs, unions and others. By the well-documented standards of past government inquiries, the review was set to be a probable whitewash – concerned with little more than optics and good PR for the Prevent programme. But crucially, those past inquiries offered at least the semblance of buy-in, or a seat at the table, for critics.

The handling of the Prevent review, meanwhile, has reflected a government intoxicated by power and indifferent to public perception. After being forced to drop the first appointee to lead the review on account of his open support for the Prevent programme, the Johnson government appointed William Shawcross – a man who has gone on record to describe 'Europe and Islam [as] one of the greatest, most terrifying problems of our future',[28] and who in his past role leading the state's Charity Commission turned it into interventionist body against Muslim-led and pro-Palestine charities.[29] Following his appointment, the review was formally boycotted by over 500 Islamic groups and organisations in Britain – a coalition which cannot be understated, constituting a historic watershed for Muslim self-organisation in Britain, and a break from the cycle of uproar, review and reconciliation that has defined antiracism for decades.

This strategy is also proving to wear thin in the sphere of policing more broadly, too. In response to the widespread deployment of Tasers, the Independent Office for Police Conduct (IOPC) initiated an investigation into police use of the weapon. In August 2021, its report was released[30] raising concerns about the discharging of Tasers in more situations that it deemed necessary. Facts highlighted included the high rate (over half) of

28 https://theguardian.com/uk-news/2021/jan/26/william-shawcrosss-selection-for-prevent-role-strongly-criticised (last accessed September 2021).
29 https://civilsociety.co.uk/news/commission-unfairly-targets-muslim-charities--says-think-tank.html (last accessed September 2021).
30 https://policeconduct.gov.uk/news/iopc-report-flags-concerns-about-police-use-taser (last accessed September 2021).

Taser discharges in incidents involving a mental health episode, as well as the racial disparities in the threat of Taser discharges. Seventeen recommendations were issued which fit neatly into the familiar mould for reports designed to have no real impact: training, guidance and community input. The report authors stated that they could not fully understand the disproportionate use of Tasers against young Black men, and called for an 'independent panel' to be set up to help them understand why this is the case.

When the IOPC report was released, Germaine Phillips, the mother of Adrian McDonald – killed in 2014 after being tasered for 24 seconds while experiencing a mental health crisis – said simply, 'It's all a stitch-up. These reports are effectively here to say: 'Well we've done that, so shut up now and go sit down.'[31] This was echoed by Carla Cumberbatch, sister of Darren Cumberbatch – killed by police in 2017 after being tasered 3 times, beaten and punched and sprayed with CS Gas – who said, 'We've already had numerous shoddy reports and unimplemented recommendations since the Macpherson review. Our families are ending up ruined from fighting for justice against a system built against us.'[32]

Upon being asked to join the IOPC's independent panel, Michael Etienne – a barrister focusing on state accountability and school exclusions – refused, citing the distinct limitations of the proposed framework for the investigation as following a decades-long pattern of impotent inquiries.[33] Police chiefs rebuffed the IOPC for proposing the investigation at all. Mean-

31 www.theguardian.com/uk-news/2021/aug/25/families-urge-ban-on-english-police-taser-use-against-people-in-distres (last accessed September 2021).

32 Ibid.

33 www.twitter.com/Metienne12/status/1430507779320602624 (last accessed September 2021).

while, following the moderate police reform agenda pushed by Theresa May, the leadership of Boris Johnson and Priti Patel have moved forcefully in favour of increased policing. Out has gone the customary odes to community policing, in has come a hard-line defence of police powers. In turn, the response from Britain's Black youth has been similarly unsentimental: the demands that surged from the Black Lives Matter demonstration were to defund or to abolish the police.

Both the forces of state violence and the forces of the street have closed ranks, and the chasm grows wider day by day.

Chapter 9

Advancing the fight?

In recent times, one question has reared its head: What organisations and organisational forms are needed to advance the struggle against racism, policing and state violence that were raised up by the likes of 2020 demonstrations? Abolitionist collectives and campaign groups against state violence – most relatively small, all undoubtedly punching above their weight – sprang into action once the demonstrations broke out. But the issue of why there was no proper existing infrastructure to channel radical, grassroots antiracist and anti-policing action was, in part, another unhappy legacy from the post-1981 period.

Government policy has increasingly outsourced the work of social control and policing to civil society organisations, redirecting them into the very architecture of violence they exist to oppose – for example, incorporating them as partners for the purposes of anti-'gang' work. Meanwhile under the banner of the 'hostile environment', homelessness charities like St Mungos have collaborated with the Home Office in the detention and deportation of homeless migrants. And the pincer move of austerity alongside the expansion of repressive 'counterterror' programmes has seen public funding dry up, while new funding streams like the Prevent programme trickle in – which serves to recruit civil society organisations explicitly into the work of monitoring 'extremism' among their communities. As a consequence, during periods of social rupture such as we are currently experiencing, civil society organisations are not simply imperfect tools but have at times become active impediments to struggle.

Meanwhile within the public sector, the Equality and Human Rights Commission (EHRC), descendant of the toothless Community Relations Commission, exists as a thoroughly moribund institution. Having been hollowed out both by the New Labour government that formed it and its conservative successors, the only times that it has crept out of terminal obscurity is when being used to advance partisan attacks on left-wing political leaders,[1] provide cover for right-wing ones[2] or when being criticised by ex-employees or ex-commissioners for 'colluding in the denial of institutional racism'.[3]

In the absence of radical institutions – be they grassroots campaign groups or mass parties – through which to articulate grievances or advance antiracist demands, such demands are instead negotiated purely through the likes of the EHRC, by appealing to the whims of workplace human resources departments, or the forces of the law. Left with such little control over their lives, individuals affected by racism are forced to invest their hopes in the good will of the powerful to alleviate their problems.

Hate crime

This is best embodied by attempts to legislate against racism, often under the rubric of 'hate crime' laws – something which follows up on the legacy of the earlier Race Relations Acts.

---

1 https://irr.org.uk/article/when-equalities-marketised-rights-suffer (last accessed September 2021).

2 https://theguardian.com/society/2020/may/12/equalities-watchdog-drops-plan-for-tory-islamophobia-inquiry (last accessed September 2021).

3 https://theguardian.com/society/2021/sep/19/britains-equality-watchdog-colluding-in-denial-of-institutional-racism and https://www.newsweek.com/equality-race-racism-ehrc-equalities-human-rights-commission-1520714 (last accessed September 2021).

From what we have outlined in this book, the question of law and order, or state violence writ large, should be chief among antiracist concerns – now more than ever. Yet through the framework of tackling hate crime, mainstream antiracist demands appear more often than not to appeal for the *expansion* of policing agencies in the name of antiracism.[4] This hate crime agenda has exploded since 2016, with organisations signing up to become hate crime reporting centres and hate crime tracker websites proliferating after the Brexit vote. But it is one that sits very uneasily with a critique of policing and state racism. The inherent deficiency of the 'hate crime' framing lies in the way it individualises and depoliticises racism and other forms of 'hate'. First by decoupling them from the institutional and structural policies of the British state and projecting them as the misdeeds of a societal fringe. Then by taking anti-hate crime work out of the sphere of movement organising and into the sphere of legal process. As indicated in the name, hate *crime* is a matter for policing, thereby re-routing the work of 'antiracism' into the arms of a British state's premier agency of racism.

While appeals to the law are perhaps understandable in the absence of organisational alternatives, the faith placed in ever-increasing hate crime laws and policing flies in the face of historical lessons over the past six decades. While proving systematically useless in addressing the racism fanned from the top of society, race hate laws have inordinately honed in on either racialised people or working-class individuals as culprits. The very first Race Relations Act (1965) was used to prosecute members of the proto-Black Power organisation Racial Adjustment Action Society (RAAS) while contemporaries like Enoch Powell MP were left unscathed. The first individual convicted

4 https://abolitionistfutures.com/latest-news/the-false-promise-of-hate-crime-laws (last accessed September 2021).

under the charge of 'racially aggravated harassment' under the Crime and Disorder Act 1998 was a Black man – fined for 'slurring' white police officers that were harassing him.[5] And prominent examples of racist 'hate crime' in the British media always seem to be committed by people of colour[6] or working-class white individuals. Such has been the bitter legacy of race laws in Britain that the Black Unity and Freedom Party included in their manifesto the demand for '[An] immediate repeal of the Race Relations Act, since it is a tool to be used against Black people'.[7]

The rolling of hate crime into the sphere of 'counterterrorism' and the government's move to regulate social media more recently also show how the emphasis on hate crime goes hand in hand with state policies of surveillance, and is becoming a pillar of the law and order project itself.[8] The 2019 report of the quasi-governmental body the Commission for Counter Extremism (CCE), 'Challenging Hateful Extremism', recommended the introduction of a broad catch-all category of 'Hateful Extremism' that blurred the line between hate, hate crime and proto-terrorist 'extremism'. Its 2021 follow-up report, 'Operating with Impunity' report, called for the greater policing of social media and the online sphere to counter 'hateful extremism'. Many on the left, particularly from already-marginalised communities, have been the target of Twitter trolling and attacks, and

5 https://independent.co.uk/news/black-is-fined-for-race-slur-on-police-insult-police-1108921.html (last accessed September 2021).

6 https://independent.co.uk/news/uk/crime/police-hunting-two-women-who-punched-muslim-woman-and-kicked-her-off-london-bus-in-islamophobic-attack-a6775081.html (last accessed September 2021).

7 https://woodsmokeblog.files.wordpress.com/2017/10/bufp-manifesto.pdf (last accessed September 2021).

8 https://tribunemag.co.uk/2021/03/the-phoney-war-on-online-hate-is-a-threat-to-the-left (last accessed September 2021).

threatening messages – yet the history of policing racism should give us pause for thought. For all the talk of tackling 'hate', such frameworks will never be used to punch upwards or adjudicate over the hate flowing from the highest echelons of society.

From delivering destruction abroad to administering the hostile environment at home, 'hate' is something the state creates and legislates everyday – how, then, could it be entrusted with preventing it? Handing over the fight against racism, misogyny or other oppressions to them would be the equivalent of drilling a hole in our lifeboats. We don't believe that campaigning for policy changes against racism is completely without merit, nor that antiracist vigilantism is a sustainable alternative to dealing with racial attacks. But vesting further powers within agencies such as the police to deal with the issue of racism only serves to expand their repertoire of powers – and leads to a perverse situation where racialised youth brutalised by police in the morning are expected to appeal to them for support against hate crime in the evening.

This emphasis on expanding hate crime powers reached its nadir in spring 2021, with calls to include misogyny as a form of hate crime mounting after the rape and murder of London woman Sarah Everard – herself killed by a serving police officer. Compounding this was the fact that these calls came alongside an increasingly assertive and violent turn by police, sanctioned from the height of government downward.

Kill the Bill

young blood
yout rebels:
new shapes
shapin

new patterns
creatin new links
linkin
blood risin surely
carvin a new path,
movin fahwod to freedom

'Movin Fowad to Freedom' – Linton Kwesi Johnson

Despite the litany of legislation pushed through in recent years to blight the lives of Black, brown and poor people, comparatively little street resistance could be summoned up in any strategic, concerted manner.

All this was to change in March 2021 with the kidnap, rape and murder of Sarah Everard by PC Wayne Couzens. Days after his arrest in March public anger grew, even before the full depravity of Couzen's actions had yet come to light. The government moved to act decidedly to quash discontent. New initiative *Reclaim the Streets* organised a vigil for Sarah – and was greeted with a swift ban. Even after challenging the decision in court the group backed down, cowed by the raw force of the state.

Thus the mantle was taken up immediately by Sisters Uncut, a radical feminist collective who continued with plans for the vigil in Clapham Common. At the vigil, row after row of police officers were deployed as woman after woman reminded the assembled crowd that Sarah's murder was an act of state violence. The point was underscored that her story fit within a wider pattern of state violence which has snatched away the lives of many from their communities. As the daylight faded the police presence intensified. And then in an instant everything shifted. Days of having their rap sheets recited back to them by the press and the public appeared to have struck a nerve with the police. Under cover of darkness the officers decided to vent their anger. Batons rained down on mourners while others were kettled and lifted away as the crowd yelled 'Shame on you!' Swiftly, political figures condemned the police response, but left the police leadership unscathed. Mayor Sadiq Khan and Home Secretary Priti Patel called for a review of the policing operation, while resisting calls to dismiss Met chief Cressida Dick. Mere days later the government would introduce the draconian Police, Crime, Sentencing and Courts Bill to Parliament – adding insult to injury and effectively rewarding police forces.

Following the scenes at Clapham Common and the unveiling of the PCSC Bill, anger rose in communities across the country – well beyond the average activist. Campaign groups including Sisters Uncut banded together as the Kill The Bill campaign, forcing the PCSC Bill out of the arcane rituals of Parliament and into public scrutiny. Meanwhile throughout Britain, police cracked down on protestors challenging the further ratcheting of state power. Nowhere was this more apparent than in Bristol, the city that lit the touchpaper that later set the streets ablaze in 1981.

Four decades later, Bristol again rebelled, initially holding a silent vigil for Sarah Everard which would see the start of a massive policing operation with protestors clubbed in the face, battered by batons and homes raided for participation in the protests. Some residents believed the violent response to be revenge for the toppling of the statue of Edward Colston into Bristol Harbour during the 2020 protests, which ignited the imagination of people around the world. When Avon and Somerset Police decided to strike back, they struck hard. Subsequent protests would be met just as violently, with some demonstrators highlighting the similarities to their experiences at the hands of the police during the 1970s and 80s. Sixty-two protestors were injured in the first night, with the official responses falsely claiming police officers had suffered broken bones and punctured lungs – a claim later retracted.

While the bill appears set to pass into law at time of writing, the campaign offers a potential model for mass organising going forward. Firstly, Kill the Bill has – despite the name – successfully avoided the trap of becoming a single-issue movement or defining its aims merely against a single provision of the PCSC Bill. By remaining resolutely opposed to the widening of policing powers, it has incorporated and mobilised around the oft-ignored discrimination facing Gypsy, Roma and Traveller (GRT) communities alongside broader issues of police brutality. It has organised direct action across distributed regional networks, and sought to build real, meaningful solidarity between otherwise isolated social and campaign groups. The latest action is Copwatch training which has trained hundreds at the time of writing in observing police interactions and how to safely intervene.

Combined with the rise of abolitionist politics over recent years, Kill the Bill has given space to nurture radical, popular politics that rejects the parochialism of campaigns of the past. The hope for the rising generation is that they are able to go even further.

Chapter 10

Reorienting the struggle

Shifting role of NGOs

In our present context, where radical institutions have undergone protracted decline while raw state power is steeply on the incline, NGOs have come to occupy an ambiguous role in social struggles. As repressive policies have come to define the political agenda, these NGOs have been forced to shift from their traditional insider-advocacy roles in Westminster to playing a more outsized role in resisting state violence.

As Britain's brutal deportation regime has become progressively insulated from popular action – for example, through the shift towards mass deportation charter flights – the fusion of popular anti-deportation action alongside NGOs has secured vital wins. The Joint Council for the Welfare of Immigrants (JCWI) began life in 1967 as an advocacy organisation conducting immigration casework, as anti-Commonwealth immigration laws began mounting. As anti-immigration laws continue to expand over half a century later, their work has grown to include judicial reviews, appeals to the Information Commissioner's Office and legal challenges against racist immigration powers. In 2020, JCWI joined with Foxglove – a non-profit specialising in algorithmic justice – to challenge the Home Office's visa streaming algorithm, under which applicants from a list of flagged 'red' nationalities would likely be denied a visa. The challenge secured the first successful judicial review of a UK algorithmic decision-making system. Yet, the response of the Home Office was a return to the norm, with Priti Patel stating her intention to look into 'unconscious bias' in the process.[1]

Meanwhile, certain elements of some of the draconian New Labour-era counterterror laws would become such a violent affront to civil liberties that they were moderated in the House of Commons. One of the most well-known is Tony Blair's plan to extend detention without charge for terror suspects to 90 days under the Terrorism Act 2006. This provision of the bill at the time received criticism across political parties and human rights organisations, with even Desmond Tutu weighing in, stating that 90 days was an 'awful deja-vu' for him, being as it was the same time limit the Apartheid regime would hold people in detention.[2] Despite calling back ministers from overseas visits to vote, Blair lost the vote with 41 of his own party's MPs rebelling in what would be the Blair administration's first major Parliamentary defeat.

Yet, the remainder of the act was passed, with many other measures that would see the ongoing erosion of democratic freedoms – not least, the fact that detention without charge remained in the police arsenal for up to 28 days. The resistance to that single provision of the act – often lauded in retellings of the period – demonstrates the limitations of a piecemeal legalistic approach to containing state power, which has itself become part of the repertoire of Antiracism from Above.

1 https://jcwi.org.uk/news/we-won-home-office-to-stop-using-racist-visa-algorithm (last accessed June 2021).

2 http://news.bbc.co.uk/1/hi/world/americas/4723512.stm (last accessed June 2021).

In the face of a deeply reactionary government hostile to any sort of progressive change, NGOs will remain an important actor – perhaps vital in the defensive struggles against criminalisation and untrammelled coercive power. But NGOs cannot *be* the movement, nor should they be expected to take on that role. In order to achieve a healthy synergy, their role must be clearly demarcated, and the terms of engagement with them should be defined alongside the wider movement.

Legalism and rights

Retreating to the language of legal rights to articulate our aims sweeps social struggles into the justice system in the hopes of defending or extending our repertoire of rights – freedom of speech, freedom of expression, freedom of association and so on.

Legal scholar Radha D'souza has written sympathetically, but powerfully, on the limitations of rights as a framework for social movements. In her words, '[The] concept of Rights does not help [activists] to reconceptualize society. When activists organize they must necessarily invoke social solidarities that are based on social relationships. Rights on the contrary focus on the relationship between state and citizens'.[3] Similarly, Shanice Octavia McBean told us that 'rights and laws are similar to the language of diversity and inclusion, in the sense one remains centred in the current hierarchy', and that as a consequence, we no longer discuss how to destroy the current political order. Aviah Sarah

3 Radha D'Souza, 'Rights, action, change: organize for what?' Aziz Choudry, Jill Hanley and Eric Shragge, *Organize: building from the local for global justice*. (Montreal: PM Press, 2012). See also D'Souza's book *What's Wrong with Rights? Social Movements, Law and Liberal Imaginations* for an in-depth assessment of the problem with the rights framework.

Day was clear that 'the law cannot be a vehicle for liberation', and pointed to the way that new laws have ended up being weaponised against the people they were meant to protect – from race relations legislation being used against Black and brown people to anti-domestic violence laws working against marginalised women.

An uncritical dependency on legal rights produces a tendency towards depoliticisation, and laws and legal processes are embedded within the domain of state power rather than undercutting it. In other words, a focus on rights keeps social struggles locked within the realm of the possible – but cannot open out onto the dreams of transformation that animated the struggles of the past. It may ameliorate the worst excesses of state violence, but cannot undermine the system that produces them. Racist techniques of policing – say, the introduction of discriminatory facial recognition technology – can be challenged through rights-based campaigns. They can be argued against on the grounds of racial discrimination, or privacy rights. But rights-based organising cannot be used to weaken policing as an institution, nor can it effectively tackle the underlying conditions of exploitation that make policing a necessary instrument for the state. Moreover, because they operate within the terms set for them by the law, campaigns framed on rights and legalism can end up legitimising unjust hierarchies when articulating their claims.

This was something that was visible in the response to the Windrush scandal in Britain. Breaking headlines in 2018, the scandal found that long-settled Caribbean citizens of the Commonwealth – the post-war 'Windrush generation' – had been falsely labelled as 'illegal immigrants' and subject to Britain's extraordinarily brutal immigration regime, up to and including deportation to countries they had not seen in decades. While public and political consensus was – rightfully – outraged at the scandal, we also saw how popular framing of the issue drew upon the particular claim of the affected individuals to Britishness, through the 'contribution' of the Windrush generation to building post-war Britain. Without undermining the fundamental merit of the cause, we can trace how pleas for justice on this basis of worthiness and belonging implicitly legitimises the detention and deportation of other groups who aren't able to place themselves within Britain's national story, or to challenge the idea that they are 'undeserving' outsiders.

Black Power-era campaigns from the Mangrove Nine to the Bradford 12 made creative use of legal rights alongside extra-court pressure to achieve their historic wins, while groups like the Asian Youth Movements operated on a model of activist-advocacy, turning cases into campaigns into causes. But defeat lingered in the wings of their victories; the legal rights they invoked were soon rolled back or written out of law by the government, and the public campaigns that secured their successes faded as Black Power made way for Antiracism from Above. Their examples should be upheld for the milestones that they were – but also as pertinent reminders that political power defines law: not the other way around.

This is certainly not to say that activists should vacate the legal sphere, ignore repressive laws or concede rights to the political right – least of all at a time when our rights are so comprehensively under attack by the government. But it does speak to the need to re-politicise our framework of rights, shifting our focus out of the matrix of state power that enshrines them and into the broader struggle for popular democracy that first defined them. It means a return to mass organising as the engine of social change. In short, we need to develop a new, politically robust framework with which to articulate our demands. We must imagine and develop new institutions to guarantee democratic freedoms. And we need to build a political culture that is able to mobilise mass popular action in defence of these – broadening outwards towards the struggle of communities, trade unions and social movements, rather than narrowing our aperture to the courts.

A little more solidarity . . .

Following Radha D'souza's line of argument to its logical conclusion offers a powerful prescription for political movements today: an emphasis on expanding social solidarities would generate new social configurations for struggles and enlarge the sphere of possibilities for political campaigns. Expanding solidarity in this way offers another path from the limiting, electorally oriented alliances that so often colour the ambitions of the left, and is a means to overcome the current impasse facing radical politics across the board. It is this very vision of solidarity that has propelled the Kill the Bill campaign – but one cannot escape the fact that, these days, solidarity appears increasingly hard to come by. We've lost count of the times that we have heard people – often younger people – declaring that 'solidarity is dead', that solidarity is an inherently undesirable concept, or that social and ethnic divisions have made antiracist solidarity 'impossible'. But solidarity is only as impossible as liberation – and unless we've overcome the conditions that demand solidarity, its obituaries are deeply premature. The fragmentation of social solidarities does, however, require serious assessment for anyone on the left.

In Chapter 7 we discussed the vexed question of 'BAME solidarity' today, and the way it has been assailed as an idea. That, in part, speaks to a growing ideological aversion to broad-based political solidarities – the transformative solidarities born of a collective commitment to socialism or internationalism. In its place has come a transactional, marketised solidarity – or an exclusive, inward-looking solidarity that is to be afforded to skinfolk alone: more a social club solidarity than a social movement one. But perhaps more important is how this turn away from solidarity is the outcome of a decades-long assault on the organisational forms through which solidarities are negotiated: from unions to community centres to political clubs. Solidarity is not found, but produced – and the political spaces through which to do so have been savaged since Thatcher's rule, and through the social alienation fostered under 40 years of neoliberalism.

Politics is nothing without organisational forms. Antiracism from Above broke up the infrastructure of Black Power and gave back 'antiracist' institutions in their place. As the politics was drained out of them, those antiracist institutions atrophied into 'equality & diversity' bodies. The decline of antiracist organisations has led some to find solace in the spontaneity and excitement of protests. Yet for others, it has led to an almost quixotic belief in the power of social media.

Over the past decade much has been written about the supposed ability of social media to democratise movements, giving the public equal opportunity to partake in strategising – and of course to coordinate demonstrations at lightning speed. And yet, the much-vaunted claim of social media being able to generate solidarity and activist bases has proved tenuous at best. While social media has done wonders to bridge geographical divides, it has done little to narrow the social gulfs opened up over the past few decades. As a medium of collective organising, it has more often than not served to reproduce the very social alienation it purports to heal – by concentrating the hostility and caprices of wider society.

In terms of antiracist organising, it shifts the focus of attention towards endless battles with opportunists and bad take-mongers online, while producing an imagined proximity to meaningful struggle. The online sphere thrives on the fire and light of Twitter storms, pile-ons or condemnatory communiques – but allows little space for the slow burn process of building solidarity. One wonders how the organisation of historic moments such as the Black People's Day of Action in 1981, if carried out today, would have confronted these tendencies so apparent across social media. Clapbacks are high-value currency in the online sphere – and we'd lie if we said we haven't indulged in them ourselves – but the level of bad faith generated by them can hinder the work of activists on the ground. Would the New Cross Massacre Action Committee be subject to shoddy trials-by-tweet in the name of 'accountability' today? Could the types of ideological divisions that existed within the community in the lead up to the Day of Action still be navigated and negotiated democratically – or would these have spilled out into bitter acrimony online?

This is before even touching on the perverse ways that social media has enabled a culture of mutual surveillance, whereby solidarity is seemingly coerced out rather than cultivated. This reaches its most absurd height with the surveillance of one another's silence: Has a prominent user condemned the latest outrage, or should their silence be read as complicity? And when it comes to the issue of unpleasant historic posts being unearthed, the cycle runs anew: Has the user issued an apology? Is the apology sufficiently sincere? And so forth. In order to disrupt organising, today's Spycops need not don a uniform and infiltrate community centres – they need only make a Twitter account. Through this dynamic, solidarity has come to be treated more as a transactional commodity to be exchanged, rather than a transformative relationship to build collective strength. And at its most grim, social media becomes an arbiter of worth – being used to determine whose struggles deserve support and whether someone, by virtue of their ethnic or social group, has or has not 'earned' the right to solidarity.

For all its promise – and perhaps partial success – of creating online 'communities' today in which to develop bonds of togetherness, social media does not so much help overcome the atomisation and alienation of our times as it does to traffic in it. There is a pressing need to replace solidaritweets with solidarity.

The present mix of organisational and ideological fissures is why, over the years, we have come to the sobering realisation that there will be no 'lightbulb moment' on the need for cross-racial solidarity in Britain. This is despite ample reminders of our racist reality: Grenfell tower, the far-right resurgence of the post-Brexit moment, the racialised impact of Coronavirus, continuous electoral success by a Conservative Party lurching ever rightward. As a priority, antiracists need to develop the organisational forms to generate durable, transformative solidarities rooted in the recognition of shared struggle – not the fragile idiosyncrasies of 'allyship' politics.

Self-organisation

At first glance, the question of solidarity sits somewhat uneasily alongside the question of the self-organisation of groups into separate caucuses within trade unions or parties, or into separate groupings entirely.

The boundary between self-organisation and 'separatism' is a subject that has never been conclusively resolved. Within popular discourse on the left, separate organising is framed as either an unconscionable affront to socialist unity or an incontestable fact of social justice. The very fact that the debate is often framed in absolutist terms precludes more delicate and nuanced discussions about the character and political programme of self-organised initiatives.

Self-organisation can be – and for some Black Power organisations, was – a means to make possible a broad-based movement for social transformation or socialism. It could ensure that multiple oppressed sections of the movement were able to join as equals alongside white (and/or male) counterparts rather than junior partners, and could develop a more stable position from which to extend solidarity to others. As Satnam Virdee framed it, '"Black" self-organisation was not a substitute for "inter-racial" class action . . . but its essential precursor'.[4]

When self-organisation is consciously adopted as part of a strategy to deepen the struggle for popular democracy for hitherto excluded social groups in this way, then it takes on a positive character. We ourselves owe our political development to political caucuses operating in the tradition of antiracist self-organisation. However, where separate organising is premised on a permanent and irreconcilable conflict between people of different identities, or is posed on the notion that different identities alone demands separation – as was the case for some other Black Power organisations – then this generates a tendency towards fragmentation. To put it another way, self-organisation can, under the right conditions and with the right aims, become the vehicle through which to negotiate from specific antiracist issues to a universalist social struggle. In the case of certain Black Power organisations, their focus on Black*

4 Satnam Virdee, 'A Marxist Critique of Black Radical Theories of Trade-Union Racism', *Sociology*, 34:3, (August 2000), pp. 545–65.

people was a means through which to construct a socialist vision that spoke to the aspirations of Black* people, rather than just speaking in their name. But if 'separation' is elevated into an ideology, rather than a strategic decision, then this creates a turn inward that weakens the broader struggle for social transformation, and can devolve into a form of sectarianism.

We therefore defend the right to self-organisation on principle, including in antiracist organising today, but would extend our support to self-organised groups on a qualified basis.

Conclusion
Recovering antiracism

Reclaiming antiracism

Alongside the crushing realities of racism, part of what radical antiracists are confronting today is an historical legacy. It is one in which Black Power in Britain was fragmented into a litany of single-issue 'antiracist' initiatives that have impeded the development of a wide-ranging radical antiracist politics.

What we term 'Antiracism from Above', then, is ultimately this strategy of containment, which was deployed to fragment and absorb the 'Antiracism from Below' represented by Black Power in Britain. Antiracism from Above was utilised to break up the radical community model of organising that underpinned the Black Power era, and to domesticate the anti-imperialist and internationalist consciousness that coursed through Black Power politics.

This served to reorient antiracist organising towards the politics of recognition – with racialised communities striving to engage the British state as stakeholders. In order to do so it promoted a tendency towards professionalisation and entrepreneurialism – as opposed to mass or popular organising – that was often underwritten by local government funding, or initiatives by sections of the Labour Party.

In periods of political weakness it is easy to be seduced by the appeal of *movementism*: a fetish for endless, eclectic, but ultimately isolated campaigns, without a strategy for transforming them into a coherent political project. Swept up in the romance of struggle, movementism offers no clear path for mediating individual struggles into a political programme, and offers no vision beyond the hope of change occurring at some indeterminate point in the future.

Meanwhile, while certain skills may be transferable from the civil society sphere into grassroots organising, but even the most well-intentioned professionals risk being trapped within the manifold illusions of civil society organising: that by 'building the brand' they are in fact 'building the movement', that by 'fine-tuning their comms' they are 'winning the public argument', or that by 'expanding their media presence' they are moving inexorably towards victory.

What, then, is the pathway through which to regenerate radical antiracism? Our prescription is in three steps: First is for an antiracist analysis that re-inserts itself within the struggles against imperialism and capitalism. Then for an antiracist praxis that reintegrates the social, political and economic facets of racism to turn it into a broader struggle for popular democracy. And finally to build this antiracism into a socialist framework for class struggle that takes as central the dynamics of race, class, gender and citizenship in order to develop a truly universalist project.

We believe that any antiracist politics that truly hopes to seize the future must be socialist – but that this is a socialist project which isn't merely able to identify an infinite number of inequities,[1] but to consolidate these into an integrated programme of class struggle.

---

1 That is to say, we wish to avoid reinforcing another type of movementism, which can support *this* struggle against racism or *that* campaign against sexism or ableism, but doesn't grapple with the question of how to bring these together in a coherent programme.

Emphasising the centrality of class struggle matters, because although the case against racism has by now obtained piercing moral clarity, we find ourselves as antiracists having to wrestle fiercely for political clarity – as much against meek tendencies of liberal antiracism as with the racists.

As such, radical antiracists must return to an antiracism rooted in the struggle of the racialised working class. Going forward we need to conclusively settle the question: is ours to be the struggle against the life-shaping realities of structural racism, or battles against the minor pains of microaggressions?

Or perhaps more importantly, with whom does our solidarity lie? Those indignant at being mistaken for the cleaner – or the cleaning workers waging heroic struggles against workplace indignities?

Reorienting towards a socialist antiracism would require a long-overdue realignment between two forces that have had a historically fraught relationship in Britain: the radical left and radical antiracists.

Just as was the case at the height of Black Power in Britain, a radical antiracist analysis spills light on the blind spots of mainstream left-wing thinking today.

Socialist antiracists argued against the grain to pierce the silences of the Labour Party left during the Corbyn years. They struggled to re-centre the battles against state violence, as their left counterparts pandered to police forces. They resisted the attempt by the mainstream left to relegate the question of radical internationalism in favour of domestic reform. They fought to recover the breadth of class politics by re-integrating issues of race and citizenship – in the face of narrow white-centred labourism.

If we recognise the many spheres through which racism is reproduced – housing, policing, schooling, the workplace and more – then antiracists should organise wherever people are in motion, from radical mass parties to trade unions to tenants unions to community defence campaigns. Antiracism should be threaded throughout all sites of social struggle rather than being 'sectionalised'.

Pondering over the question, Aviah Sarah Day depicted a broad-ranging vision of antiracism which – crucially – seeks to move beyond small wins, and control the levers of power:

> What I want to see is organising around immigration, school exclusions, prisons and policing more linked up with workers and tenants struggles to seize control of the means of production...[It's] important that it's connected to building dual power so whether tenants organising for rent reductions and seize housing or workers organising for pay & conditions to eventually seizing those workplaces – these are the organisational forms that work.[2]

The sharp criticism levied against mainstream British trade unions by Black Power groups were powerful and compelling. In many ways, they remain valid: one need only look at how effortlessly major trade union figures have been willing to throw migrants under the bus, or the example of the GMB union agitating for Britain's Trident nuclear programme in the name of giving 'stability and security to [British] jobs and communities', to see that British chauvinism still has a home in the trade union movement.[3]

But there is a qualitative difference between arguing against integrating within trade unions in 1970s Britain – at the height of their powers – and today, at an historic low point.

2 Day, Aviah Sarah, *WhatsApp* voice note message to Ilyas Nagdee.

3 http://archive.gmb.org.uk/newsroom/gmb-on-trident-renewal-vote (last accessed September 2021).

Gargi Bhattacharyya gave us a clear and unsentimental perspective on the need for people of colour to organise within trade unions, despite them seeming unpromising and with their leadership all-too-willing to compromise: 'Longstanding organisations such as unions retain an infrastructure that is necessary to utilise if we are [to] extend antiracist struggle and to cement connections between different elements of social justice movements.'

If we want a socialist antiracism rooted in the struggles of the racialised working class, then that necessarily means struggling within the institutions that are, for all their faults, integral to development of working-class power in Britain.

A shift to trade unionism needn't, however, mean an uncritical return to a 'classic' trade union model frozen in time, nor does it mean recapitulating to the parochial workerist ideas of some of its leadership. It is in this context where the issue of self-organised caucuses becomes particularly salient.

Meanwhile the defiant unionism of the United Voices of the World (UVW) and Independent Workers of Great Britain (IWGB) unions has convulsed the British labour movement with their dynamism and militancy. Largely comprising non-white and migrant workforces in sectors like the service sector and gig economy workers, these unions have intervened forcefully to organise the most exploitable section of the workforce – and to harness their explosive potential.

Trade union campaigning branching outward from workplaces to support social struggles for housing, infrastructure and localised battles would also help reinvigorate unionism, and defy the simple dichotomy between community and workplace.

Day highlighted how, contra the idea that workers struggles and antiracist struggles are distinct from one another, they have been at their most powerful when they have been mutually reinforcing.

The British left overcoming their narrow economism and embracing a radical antiracist perspective, therefore, is doing no favours for Black and brown people. Rather, it would be rooted in the understanding that there is no anti-capitalist future that does not recognise race as one of the central means through which capitalism reproduces itself – and that the struggles of the migrants and racialised working class strike at the cornerstone of the system.

Radical antiracist praxis is how socialism gets its soul back.

Rebuilding community

Building up those social struggles requires an organised presence within racialised communities, to give political expression to their simmering discontent.

Gargi pointed to the organisational diversity of antiracist struggles : 'I do think UK antiracism has had many homes – and that most of the community homes remain unrecognised in the larger movement and have been poorly documented'.

When we spoke to Adam Elliott-Cooper he warned against the tendency among the left to register only some easily-recognisable forms of struggle as 'political', while discounting the political character of, for example, the anti-police uprisings of 2011.

In an article for Novara Media marking a decade since those rebellions, Elliott-Cooper highlighted the clearly political precursors and aftermath to the uprisings – from the spate of deaths in police custody that set the tone of the summer before Mark Duggan's killing, as well as the community-led defence campaigns that emerged afterwards to support youth subject to draconian sentences.[4]

According to Elliott-Cooper, an analytical lens that only sees 'politics' taking place within a narrow frame, does a disservice to those people that are forced to articulate their politics in different ways. And it risks excluding the political expressions of some of the most oppressed sections of Britain's working class: women, migrants and its downwardly racialised strata.

As he says, 'If we want to bring new people in, we need to recognise the civil participation that oppressed people engage in and rebellions are part of that.' The community-rooted campaigns of groups like the Northern Police Monitoring Project, 4Front Project and London Campaign Against Police & State Violence provide a critical means of organising and giving political clarity to those communities.

In a more holistic sense, 'Community' was central to the work of Black Power organisations – providing the circulatory system through which their radical visions could be developed, deliberated and disseminated.

But across Britain, those spaces and places that were once the beating heart of radical communities-in-motion have today been swept away by urban transformation, or atrophied in the face of social change.

The former site of the Mangrove restaurant in London's Kensington lies in the shadow of Grenfell tower – whose charred husk stands as a solemn emblem of gentrification, racism and class power in one of Britain's most unequal boroughs.

To its east lies Tower Hamlets, whose Council continues to support history and heritage projects catered towards the Bangladeshi community, while simultaneously presiding over

4 https://novaramedia.com/2021/08/03/10-years-after-the-riots-the-left-is-finally-taking-on-the-police-state (last accessed September 2021).

'redevelopment' plans forcing those communities out of the borough.

Moss Side, where the Manchester Black Women's Co-op was formed, faces down its own gentrification threat today. Meanwhile Handsworth, Birmingham's historical tinderbox and former home of the Harriet Tubman bookshop lies in an inner ring of decay, dilapidation and concentrated poverty encircling the city centre.

To be able to struggle *with* our communities, we now need to struggle *for* the very survival of those communities.

Inspiring acts of community resistance have fired our imagination – from the mass neighbourhood protest in Glasgow that halted immigration vans in their tracks, to the mutual aid networks developed as the pandemic began, to ACORN, London Renters Union and other tenants' unions across the country building power at the very root of communities.

But we don't believe that a move towards community organising means downscaling our ambitions, depoliticising our aims or turning away from the dream of social transformation. The onward march of gentrification across urban centres in Britain today underlines the fact that we cannot afford a simple retreat from the state into small social cliques, but must reshape state power in its entirety.

If anything, perhaps today's community strategies should more closely resemble the type of grand ambitions that the Black Liberation Front outlined in their pamphlet on Revolutionary Black Nationalism:

> Self-determination or black control of black communities is a reasonable objective *provided that it does not rest there* . . . Community control would mean an *organisation that is powerful enough to exist as a parallel government* in the Black commu-

> nity, and effective enough to virtually replace the national government (emphasis added).[5]

Recovering internationalism

As part of a realignment between the forces of the left and antiracists, socialist antiracists must refuse the British left's historical dereliction of duty: its compromise with imperialism and its rejection of radical internationalism.

Antiracists today must combat the generation-long effort to nullify the radical internationalism of past antiracist movements. At a time when social and labour struggles in Britain are slowly increasing, activists here are bound by the solemn duty to evade the pitfalls of decades past – to pierce through the ideological brick wall that separates *our* struggles from those of people in the Global South, or which compartmentalises international solidarity as merely optional.

Ours is a solidarity that must extend throughout the supply chain. The support afforded to retail workers being exploited on the shop floor here must be extended backwards to the sweatshop worker in Ethiopia producing the garments, to the agricultural worker in India producing the raw material, and the communities in Bangladesh whose waterways run jet black with industrial pollutants.

The work of direct-action groups like Palestine Action has been integral in drawing out and organising against the British state and British capital's web of complicity with apartheid. Similarly, anti-raids and anti-deportation campaign groups have, in the course of challenging inter-state deportation arrangements for local campaigns, been forced to confront Britain's role in the

5 'Revolutionary Black Nationalism: A paper for discussion', WONG/6/40, *Papers of Ansel Wong*, held at: London: Black Cultural Archives.

international system. International solidarity campaigns organised alongside people's movements and radical governments across the Global South are also central to the development of a meaningful international solidarity that can translate moral support into material.

But ours should also be an international solidarity that penetrates through ruling class duplicity, and their attempts to redefine internationalism to serve their own ends. Before troops had even left Afghanistan in August 2021, British politicians – seized of their own self-importance – debated how best to restore Britain's reputation on the international scene. Familiar odes to that other strain of internationalism soon followed, with invocations of women's rights and battles against authoritarianism peppering the discourse.

Therefore in striving for a radical internationalism, we must also recover the ideas that animated the radical internationalism of yesteryear: questions of national liberation, sovereignty for the Global South, social and economic transformation, and the centrality of imperialism. It should be an internationalism that moves away from the paternalism of international NGOs, or the moralism of Human Rights internationalism, towards a holistic framework of liberation. And it should organise with and alongside peoples' movements and radical governments to allow the people of the South to struggle on their own terms, rather than impose our will upon them.

Those of us residing in the viper's nest of imperial power in the West have a double responsibility to ensure that our internationalism does not give free license for our governments to pillage the Global South. While recovering a radical internationalist perspective to infuse into our antiracism, ours must be an international against imperialism.

Making them afraid again

By 2020 we were well acquainted with overcast skies.

We had both spent years marching under them to tiny demonstrations against this act of police violence or that racist outrage, buffeted by rain or blanketed by steel grey clouds. We had attended protests ignored by the media, joining solemn chants drowned out by the din of society.

But even then, this book began life at a time when the horizon seemed unfathomably dark. We were still stinging from the disaster of the 2019 election, settling in for the COVID pandemic, while seeing misery consume people across the world: the ongoing tragedy of the Palestinians, the fresh cruelty facing the Bolivians.

Amid this, the Black Lives Matter demonstrations burst through like a blaze of sunlight in May. The tiny demonstrations against police violence that we were used to became mass revolts that swarmed the centres of power in Britain. The names we had chanted solemnly in memory became rallying cries ringing out across the country. The comrades that had long moved heaven and earth against injustice were thrown from darkness to the dazzling light of TV cameras. In a word: 'antiracism' had become popular again.

The cogs of power soon began turning once more, setting in motion some familiar strategies. 'Antiracism' was being spilled across magazine pages and beckoned onto award show stages. Newfound 'leaders' were being picked, polished and paraded before our eyes. The more expansive ambitions of the rebellions were being scaled back into single-issue 'equality' causes.

And yet, our allegiances remain with the struggles of the shadows. The antiracism we speak of belongs to the brutalised people who refuse to shrink from the policeman's gaze. To the deaths-in-custody campaigners that sink months, years or decades in pursuit of justice. And to the migrant workers whose militancy keeps their bosses awake at night.

But the struggles that we have taken greatest inspiration from are those that are sweeping in their conception of both space and time. From the radical internationalists of the Palestinian liberation struggle who understood their campaigns as one in a constellation of global injustices, to the Chilean people, the first children of neoliberalism, steeled by insight that their struggle was not about 30 pesos, but about 30 years.

Reflecting the zeitgeist of the times, Black Power groups of twentieth century Britain radiated an infectious – perhaps even over imaginative – radicalism, which was conscious of its place in a global geography of resistance. But if they could be faulted for an excess of ambition, today we would certainly be faulted for a dearth of it. The question facing us is how to develop a radical antiracist programme that keeps apace with the breathtaking speed of social change.

What we need is an antiracism that reclaims its rightful place as the tip of the spear for socialism. What we need is an antiracism infused with the worldmaking ideals of history's most potent struggles. Perhaps, above all, what we need is an antiracism that makes those in power afraid again.

Thanks to our Patreon subscribers:

Andrew Perry
Ciaran Kane

Who have shown generosity and comradeship in support of our publishing.

Check out the other perks you get by subscribing to our Patreon – visit patreon.com/plutopress.

Subscriptions start from £3 a month.